MAJOR HERBERT R. HOSKINS MC

THANK YOU MISTER BOSH

THAT'S CLOSE ENOUGH!

EXTRACTS FROM LETTERS HOME
FROM THE SOMME, 1915-1916

MAJOR HERBERT R. HOSKINS MC

THANK YOU MISTER BOSH

THAT'S CLOSE ENOUGH!

EXTRACTS FROM LETTERS HOME
FROM THE SOMME, 1915-1916

Major Herbert R. Hoskins MC
1st/7th Battalion
Royal Warwickshire Regiment

Compiled and edited by his grandson
John R Hoskins with Frances Hoskins, 2013

MEREO
Cirencester

Published by Mereo

Mereo is an imprint of Memoirs Publishing

25 Market Place, Cirencester, Gloucestershire, GL7 2NX
info@memoirsbooks.co.uk www.memoirspublishing.com

Thank you Mr Bosh, that's close enough!

ISBN: 978-1-86151-027-3

INTRODUCTION

When I was at school we were not taught about the horrors of the First World War. On Saturday 29th July 1916 Grandpa writes 'I have revenged my pals. It is a great feeling to have the Bosh running away in front of you. I can't tell you anything now but some day I will'.

It is however, a well-known fact that men of my grandfather's generation who had fought in that conflict did not talk about their experiences, and although I was very close to Grandpa, I never asked - and oh, how I wish I had.

These extracts about his daily life on the Somme in 1915 and 1916 have been lying in a drawer, and I did not read them properly until these last few months. My wife Frances, who found them as interesting as I did, has enthusiastically helped me to create what we hope is a simple but effective memorial to my grandfather and to my Great Uncle Cyril, who perished on 1st July, 1916.

It may read differently from other wartime diaries perhaps, for not only does it demonstrate the horror of war, it also displays the bravery and the resilience of those fighting men together with their tears, sadness and the rare opportunities for fun and some laughter.

Grandpa entered the war in 1914, having joined up as a Territorial. He rose from 2nd Lieutenant to Major. He was awarded the Military Cross in 1917 in the King's

Birthday Honours' List. Following a period of instruction at Witham, Essex with the Royal Warwickshire Regiment, his Battalion departed from Southampton on 22nd March, 1915 on the SS Copenhagen and SS City of Lucknow bound for Le Havre. The official War Diary notes that the Battalion consisted of 30 officers, 1003 men, 23 vehicles and 78 horses. This book portrays his daily life during the conflict.

John Hoskins 2013

Prior to departure for France, 1914

Portrait of Major Hoskins in 1918

THE DIARY

MONDAY MARCH 22ND 1915:
BASINGSTOKE STATION 12.5 P.M.

We left Witham at 7.30 am as arranged. I got up at 3 am having had three and a half hours sleep in my clothes on a couch at Mr. Pullen's. Going along very slowly - seem to be sticking here. It's raining hard so looks like being cheery if we go on board today. Am fairly tired just now, still I shall have plenty to do to keep me awake. We do not know for sure when we leave. The second train will catch us up at this rate.

Wednesday 24th March 6.25 pm

Just a line to say I am A1 and going strong. We left the boat at 2.30 pm yesterday and left for camp at 4 pm. Had to go up a tremendous hill with three twists to get up. I was able to get the horses down between 8 or 9 pm and then got some sleep. I was awake and up at 6 am and after a good amount of hard work left camp with the Battalion at 12 noon. It rained all night, but we were in tents with wood boards, so were quite comfy. We left the station at 5 pm. I am now in a kind of luggage truck, known as the Stores. I shall certainly put some straw down soon and sleep as it is getting dark. I can't say where we are off to although I know, but of course we are all on our honour not to say. We expect to be on the train for 24 hours. Passing through very pretty countryside.

I was Officer in Charge of troops on the ship and was told we disembarked very well in record time and quicker than usual.

Too dark to write more. I'm quite well and happy. Ring up home and give them my love.

Thursday 25th March 11.35 am

Still on the train. Have been sleeping and eating all day. Managed to shave but not wash. Still raining - had quite a good night's rest. Have heard of Cyril* but not seen

* FOOTNOTE: Herbert's younger brother Lt. Cyril Hoskins, $1^{st}/8^{th}$ Batt. Royal Warwickshire Regiment, born 1890, mobilised August 1914. Killed in the Somme battle 1st July, 1916 as described later. His name is recorded on the Thiepval Memorial.

him - he's helping the 6th transport officer. Passed through country swarming with magpies - largest rookery I've ever seen.

Friday 26th March

Going strong - came to rest last night and have not moved since.

Saturday 27th March 2.30 pm

Topping day sunshine and quite warm. Have plenty of work to keep me on the move, I can tell you. I am ready for sleep at night. Saw some of the other transport today, they have all had a rough time - one has killed two horses and broken a wagon or two. With the exception of colds my horses are well - some still have sores they received on board or rail. I have repaired the brakes etc. so that we can get a move on in decent safety again. Get well worried at times but all seems to straighten out after a while.

Monday 29th March 7.10 pm

I have had four letters from you yesterday and today and there are two bags in the orderly room so I expect I shall get another from you tomorrow.

Tuesday 30th March

Had no time to finish off yesterday. We are 160 miles from where you heard of Cyril★. I did not see him there but have done so two or three times since. He looks A1. Here's breakfast - so half a mo.

The Battalion are out digging so am spending the time pulling my transport together. Have you sent any 'baccy' out yet as I am out of all I brought?

Friday April 2nd 2.30 pm

Getting a letter each post. We are close up to the line now and can hear the guns and rifle fire plainly. Three bombs fell last night just after we arrived. We do not know for sure how long we shall be here.

It's a topping place and I have a good billet. The people here have left and a man and wife are in charge. There is a bath! All gas and water is cut off, but every house seems to have a pump. Nearly all the civilians here live downstairs and the military use the top. My 'gees' are all better today - if we stay here a few days I shall get most of them well again. Must get on parade now.★★

★ *FOOTNOTE: The Territorial Battalions (1st/5th, 1st/6th, 1st/7th and 1st/8th) proceeded to France at the end of March 1915, and following training at Bailleul, went into the trenches in that district south of Ypres. In July they were sent south to Courcelles, and after further training they went again into the trenches near Hébuterne before Gommecourt. They remained in that district, with billets at Fonquevillers, until June 1916.*
The battalion route-marched to Granville and on to billets at Winnezeele on the Belgium French border. By 30th March they were in Bailleul and transported by bus to the vicinity of Neuve Eglise and Damoutre, where they were engaged in digging trenches.

★★ *FOOTNOTE: The battalion route-marched to Armentières and Houplines to 'look around the trenches and learn the routine'. This would appear to be a time of general instruction.*

THE MAPS OF THE AREA
THE BATTLEFIELDS OF THE SOMME

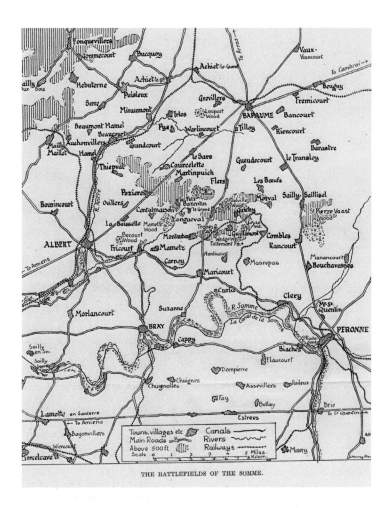

THE BATTLEFIELDS OF THE SOMME.

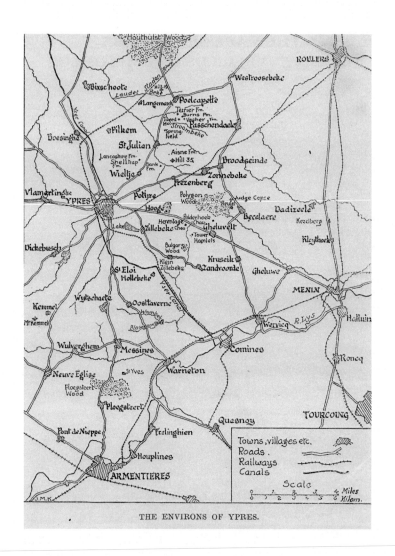

Houthulst Wood

ROULERS

Bixschoote

Westroosebeke

Laudet

Langemarck Poelcapelle

Tellier Fm.
Burns Fm.
Vapher Fm.
Ho.Stroo Passchendaele
Springbeke
field

Boesinghe Pilkem

St Julian

Lancashire Fm.
Shell trap
Bank
Fm.

Aisne Fm.
Hill 35

Broodseinde

Wieltje

Zonnebeke

Vlamertinghe YPRES

Frezenberg

Potijze

Polygon
Wood

Judge Copse

Dadizeele

Hooge

Polderhoek
Chau.

Becelaere

Kezelberg

Lake Zillebeke

Herenlage
Chau.

Gheluvelt

Kleythoek

Tower
Hamlets

Dickebusch

Bulgar
Wood

Klein
Zillebeke

Kruseik
Zandvoorde

Gheluwe

St Eloi
Hollebeke

Wytschaete

Oosttaverne

MENIN

Kemmel

Mt Kemmel

Wambek

Blauwpoort

Wervicq

R. LYS

Halluin

Wulverghem

Messines

Comines

Roncq

Neuve Eglise

St Yves

Warneton

Ploegsteert
Wood

Ploegsteert

Quesnoy

TOURCOING

Pont de Nieppe

Frelinghien

Houplines

ARMENTIERES

J.M.K.

Towns, villages etc.
Roads.
Railways
Canals

Scale
0   1   2   3   4 Miles
0 1 2 3 4 5 6 Kilom.

THE ENVIRONS OF YPRES.

6

Saturday 3rd April 10.10 am

Has begun to rain - first time for some days - hope it will not last long. Have to go round to the other transports now and see if all is correct. Hope there will not be anything too bad - I do not believe so.

Easter Sunday April 4th 2.45 pm

I have just read your Wednesday letter. We have not had any post for two or three days until today - there may be some more from you yet, as all the bags have not been looked through yet. The Company Officer censors the men's letters, no one the officers' (thank goodness).

Where we are I cannot tell you.* We are certainly not in Germany! As to food we get heaps - and good. Have asked Mother to send a cake once a week as home-made cannot be bought. This is a fairly large town - something like Leamington or Warwick.* We hear guns all day and night. Most of the officers and men have been in the trenches for instruction 24 hours at a time by half companies. A few shells drop in the town now and again, otherwise things are as quiet as they might be at home.

I have quite a comfy billet. The folk have left, so our servants do everything for us. Can get a hot bath and washing done here. I am having a slack time the last two days as little transport is required. Today is very still.

*FOOTNOTE: The War Records show the Battalion were in Armentières, on the border between France and Belgium, in wet and miserable weather.

7

Several of us went to a Communion Service at 8 am today. Our Parson (Macready) took it in a large room which has been shelled at some time.

I inspected all the Brigade lines yesterday - all correct. It takes a day to get to everybody as they have all have heaps of questions and want to know how each is getting along. I made a few suggestions for extra comfort for the horses etc.

Had Auster of the 8th here for lunch today. He's quite fit. It's quite a regular Sunday today the slackest day since we left Witham.

We have had one casualty so far. Yesterday a fellow was cooking bacon in the trenches and a shell exploded nearby, cutting his face - but not too bad.

Things are at a deadlock here at present. The trenches are quite the best on the Line. I have not been in yet and do not know if I shall go. It is not necessary for me to do so - still I'd like to see them.

One gets quite used to hearing the guns - the only thing that worried me last night was a wretched dog that would keep howling.

You can see folk walking the streets in their Sunday best as if nothing was happening.

I am quite happy and as safe as possible. Also very much enjoying it all!

Monday April 5th 2 pm

We move off again tomorrow - back to our last place having finished our instruction here. The Battalion we have been attached to would like us to remain, as they say we are the smartest Battalion they have had to instruct - so one up to us!*

We have had three casualties only and none very bad. I should like to stay here longer as it is a much larger and nicer place than the other.

Thursday 8th April 2.40 pm

Am just as fit as a fiddle now and quite enjoying life. I am just off to see the 6th and 8th after seeing Major Goode who should be here at 2.30 to see the ASC horses.

I do not get much night work - in fact none to mention and long nights. I sleep from 9 to 7 am.

Today I got up at 7 am, had a cup of coffee, washed, shaved etc. Had a look at the horses and then breakfast. Then stables. I arranged for an NCO and 16 men to have riding school.

This afternoon I visited the 6th and 8th to see if their harness and wagons were all correct and sent in the weekly report.

I saw the 5th yesterday. That made it five o'clock. Had some tea and then went round the horses and saw the sick ones attended to.

We dine at 7 o'clock!

I will just go round to see one sick 'gee' and then turn in.

*FOOTNOTE: The Battalion received instructions to march to Bailleul for training to continue. This route march was much harassed by motor lorries. On arrival they found very unsatisfactory and insanitary conditions. A complaint was made. They proceed to tidy up the billets. Grandpa comments that the Battalion always had to clean up the billets allotted to them before they were fit for occupation.

Friday 9th April 8.55 pm

Have just finished dinner and a jolly good one too. We had mutton, 'taters, leeks etc. followed by stewed figs, some plovers' eggs (which had been sent to the Colonel), egg omelette, chocolate biscuits and a whisky and soda. Not bad.

I spent most of the morning looking to the horses, which as a whole are much better. This afternoon I was with Morgan of the 1/6th searching for the vet. We rode several miles and were lucky to get him just as he was moving away, so have arranged to get him here at 9.30 to see mine and then take him round to the other three Battalions.

There is not much to do at present - just routine work and we expect to be moved again any time next week. I do not know where to - no one does.

I saw Cyril today. He has a cold in both eyes. He's been on a bomb-throwing course with many officers from each Battalion.*

I have to sit down and censor the men's letters now. Thank good goodness they do not write very much.

I had a letter from Dad today and a postcard from Pops - all seem well.

Folk here do not seem to expect the war will last very long. I hope they are right and we shall be home playing tennis before the season is over. Ye gods, what a time. I shall not want to start work for a few weeks, I know. This is really in a way a slack job up to the present - we have had a few very stiff days, but all round not like ordinary days in and out of work.

*FOOTNOTE: The course was in Armentières.

Tuesday 13th April 10.40 pm

I am having quite a new experience just now. I'll give you the last two days' doings. Sunday as you know by now I received orders to move the following day. The Battalion fell-in at 8.50 am, A, B, C, D Companies in that order followed by transport. Each Battalion marched on its own. We were not brigaded. I left two sick horses and one mare that had foaled Sunday. Two as I have told you died Sunday making 5 in all and my total in shortage is now 7. As I have two mules too many I am only three down.

On the way here - not many miles - eight or nine - we were held up for two hours or more because the Germans were shelling where we wanted to pass. The cheek of it!

Our Battalion took over some trenches from a regular Battalion last night. Well - we got to a rest farm (say three miles back from the trenches which are on the other side of a hill) at about 4 o'clock. At least the Battalion did, including the two water carts, Medical Officers and mess carts and cooks, wagons. I left the Battalion a mile before with all the other wagons and came here to my lines with the QM.

We are about 87 men here all told - Transport 50. I started off to go to the Battalion but got sent back for the baggage wagons - two - so the blankets and officers' kits could be issued. That took half an hour. Then I brought back all that was left on the wagons.

After a while my sergeant turned up with coke, so off we went to the Battalion again. Owing to other

11

transport we missed them, so we had to take it to the 'dumping ground' - that is the Battalion HQ when the Battalion is in the trenches.

Flares kept going up and stray bullets whizzed over our heads - all high up. When I got there the QM was there with the other wagons, so between us we got the stuff dumped and arrived back here at 12.30 am

While out we had two limbered wagons in ditches and the ditches are anything up to 4 ft. deep. The roads are very bad. You are only allowed one way on most roads, they are so narrow. The Sergeant and I with a driver and two horses got all clear but it was quite a game while it lasted.

All in the dark of course - one cannot go to the dumping ground in day time when a Battalion is in the trenches.

We fed and got to bed at 2 am. Breakfast was at 8 or 7 am, but I forget which. After that I went with the QM to draw forage, coke, letters and papers. I had read yesterday's London Mail by 10 am today.

I got back at 12.30 pm and saw the stables. This afternoon I helped with a 'dugout' used for harness etc. that was nearly finished by the gang we followed.

After tea I went and fetched wood, wire, sandbags, nails etc. from Brigade HQ. Captain Lea, whom you met with me just outside Caledon one Sunday, came in to tea yesterday. At 7 pm we waited outside the rest farm for it to get dark - then got along to the dumping ground

It was a merry night - plenty of bullets about. I was glad to get away again as I expected a horse to be hit any minute. I was back here about 9 pm. Captain Jones the QM looked after the food going up. Then yesterday we had food at eight. It was a dirty day with rain.

I went into a town nearby and got bread, wine and several things for here, the Colonel and fellows in the trenches and it took me all morning. I also drew 125 FRS from the Field Cashier - you see we are all right for cash.

Auster came in for tea. I left at 5 to fetch the RE stuff from HQ. They said there was not much but when I reached there, to my delight there was a good wagon load of stuff so I had to borrow a wagon to draw some of it here, then change it into one of mine, so we delayed some time and didn't leave here until 8.30 pm.

The QM had gone with four limbered wagons. I took a new road and took a fellow who went that way the night before as a guide. Blowed if he hadn't forgotten and took us 600 yards past our turning. It was all right as it happened and we were able to turn. Then just as we go to the DG the wretched ASC driver got his wagon into a ditch. So I went on.

I was in the mess cart with the stuff I had bought during the morning and I got two horses, an NCO and 20 men to unload the wagon - pulled it on to the road, loaded up again and drew on down to the DG..

I had some apples for the Colonel - he's very fond of them - also Jones had some milk for him so he was quite pleased to see us. I took some of the boys two fresh loaves, some wine and fresh milk. They look forward to us now. We got back here at 1.30 am.

During the day we are getting ready food, letters, coke etc. to take up after dark.

Tomorrow our Battalion comes out and we go to where the 6th are for four days, so we shall only have two more nights to go up to the DG. (Dumping Ground). *

I am feeling as fit as possible and ready for lunch. We are waiting for the 'taters to boil. Feeding is A1. I look like getting as fat as butter - it is only extras like cake etc. that one enjoys but are not necessary to keep one fed that we miss. Bacon and eggs for breakfast, roast beef for lunch, plenty of jam, butter and marmalade, tea, sugar, fresh milk. The latter we have to buy along with eggs.

As to casualties - up to date we have had none killed and at the outside half a dozen wounded.

Friday 16th April 5.35 pm

We have had no letters today as there has been a smash down the line, which caused a block. Hope they get it cleared quickly.

I have had a name put over the door of our farm - 'The Constitutional Club - Witham City' and we call this Witham Camp. We have that up on a large board on the road so you see we feel quite at home. There are camps known as Aldershot, Bulford, Port Arthur etc. and in time they get to be known by these names.

I am off to the DG to fetch the Battalion out - they are relieved by the 8th tonight.

FOOTNOTE: The Battalion left Bailleul for the vicinity of Plougsteert. They were delayed 2½ hours en route owing to heavy shelling of the road. They remained at a farm named Courte Dreve for some four hours and then proceeded to the trenches after dark. 'The trenches are in very poor condition and will require a lot of work to make them safe.' The enemy was in position on the slopes of Messines Hill near Hill 60. Captain Hoskins reports that they will have to do much work joining up the trenches which are at present disconnected.

The QM and transport wagons have just gone. I shall follow in the mess cart. I need not go really but I am sure to find something to do there and I like to see the fellows.

Very still today - and has been for the last few days. Our chaps have only to hold the enemy - there is not much use firing a lot as we cannot advance until the two flanks come up.

When you go up at nights you see lights, flares, shells all around. There was another aeroplane show tonight - we can easily see them being shelled. You see several puffs of smoke all around the plane but still she sails gaily along. They are a very hard target.

I arrived back at 1 am last night and shall be late again I expect tonight. Am leaving at 6.45 pm.

Am fit and smiling - get ready for me at the end of this summer.*

Saturday 17th April 2 pm

We got the fellows out all right last night but very late The 8th boxed things up badly and instead of my leaving trench HQ by about 10 o'clock I left with the last wagon at 2 am and got here in daylight about 4.15.

Fellows tell of near things such as one had a bullet through his pack on his back and was not touched. Another lost half his whiskers and no further harm done. Another had his hat shot through etc.

It was a very dark night - pitch black.

Am A1 today — just off to go up to Rest Headquarters - 2 miles away.

* FOOTNOTE: The Battalion were in the trenches south of Messines Hill.

Sunday 18th April 4.40 pm

Have just had tea and am eating a piece of Captain Jones chocolate I've just bagged. All eatables are public property between us. By now you will be hearing what I do when Battalion is in the trenches and when out I get almost the same job but - and a big BUT - during the daytime I am as happy as can be singing, laughing and ragging the interpreter. He's a wretched worm and it's a job to make him understand at times.

As you may know, all sale of whisky has been stopped so I've been sending him to get some from private houses. He says though he'll not go for any more as he is liable to be sent to prison. He's right - but by gum, he's weak hearted. I'll bet I get some and shan't go to prison! The Colonel wants it as he has always been used to it, so I'll have to keep him supplied somehow.

I got hold of two dozen bottles last night. I'd not a penny left yesterday of the 125 francs I drew two or three days ago. All spent on stuff for Companies. I drew it back today. It all adds to my day's work and is not part of my allotted job. The Colonel thanked me for doing it and said I'd done jolly well, so that's good.

I went up to Headquarters today before lunch and found a service just beginning so I stayed for communion too - not three miles from the German trenches. We sang two hymns and guns kept popping all the time.

I am now going to have a few rounds with the gloves for the fun of it.

I sent Cyril one bottle of whisky, a loaf of bread, a bottle of milk and four eggs. Gave them to his transport officer to take up. I learn from Lt. Ash, who saw Cyril last night, that he's quite well.

Monday 19th April 8.40 pm

The 7th relieve the 8th tomorrow, so shall begin night work again tomorrow evening. Today has been very peaceful up to now and a lovely day. I was out all morning getting things for the officers and delivering them this afternoon. Also the cash. I make them pay up before they go into the trenches.

'B' Company made a fuss about things - at least Ash, their Mess President, did - so they can go without for a while! I do not bother myself for their comfort and stand to lose by it into the bargain if they make any row. They can jolly well look after themselves.

I've arranged for each company to let me have a list of what they require and I get as much of it as I can. It means that with our mess here I have six separate accounts to look after. It is good to see their faces when I arrive with the stuff.

I'm as fit as possible and as happy as a sandboy.*

Tuesday 20th April 1.15 pm

We take our Battalion into the trenches again tonight* and it looks like being a decent one too. Jolly hot again.

* FOOTNOTE: *The Battalion was in the Petit Pont area*

I took my 'gee' out this morning and he got a nasty cut somewhere on the way - just above the fetlock so I shall have to rest him for a day or two.

I feel just like a good laze on the river at Stratford upon Avon.

Oh - I have got the mare we lost at the last place back again - and a man is fetching the one that foaled back here so I shall only be one short. Good-oh.

Wednesday 21st April 1.50 pm

We got the Battalion into the trenches all right last night - in fact Jones and I were back here by 10 o'clock. We went to the Trench Dump, cleared the wagons and were away before of the 8th transport arrived or any of their men out of the trenches.

I should say they would all be clear by 10 or 11 instead of 3 am as they were the day the 8th relieved us.

I'm going to see Cyril now - they are at the place we cleared out of last tonight. The 5th are handy, not far along this road in huts.**

I saw Jack Cooper and some of the boys this morning. Stopped and had a few words. They had not cleared up after coming out last night.

Guess I'll be seeing Leslie tonight.

We do not leave until 7 pm now as it is too light - almost like daylight last evening and very still. I only noticed one shot go over my head.

It was good to see Leslie and Cyril tonight.

FOOTNOTE: The Battalion took over the trenches - known as the Steenbeck trenches - from the 1st/8th RW.

**FOOTNOTE: The Battalion searched local farms in the early morning for snipers. They remained near the Steenbeck trenches until 30th April.*

Thursday 22nd April 11 pm

The weeks soon roll by out here. Our fellows come out on Saturday and I hope the 8th get in a little sharper this time.

Friday 23rd April 3.20 pm

I have just been reckoning up how much I am owed by various Messrs. It comes to 198.50 Frs. I had better get hold of that when they all come out tomorrow.

I have bought myself a pair of cloth slippers to wear at night and jolly nice they are too.

Nothing of any interest has happened around here this week so far. The ping-pong goes on and away on our left there is some heavy fighting judging by the sounds we can hear. Our lines keep the same - one or two fellows get sniped each night but fortunately only small wounds and no one killed.

I am going to visit Leslie now as he is just 400 yards away. I expected him here before this. The men get plenty to do when our of the trenches so I expect he's been too busy to get away.

Oh dear - it looks like being a rotten night and I think we will get some rain. I suppose I should not grumble - we have had only one wet night here so far.

Murray Junior is here at present. He came back early from the trenches to go to a bomb-throwing course. He arrived about 5.30 am and lay down beside me. He came back to lunch and has had a bath and gone to bed as he cannot get back before dark so he will go with us at 7 pm.

Jones and I had baths yesterday in a large round tub and very splendid it was too; we have not had a bath for two or three weeks. Topping hot water too.

Saturday 24th April 6.15 pm

I will fetch the Battalion out tonight and will leave here at 7 pm so should be back about 12 midnight or so. The nights are very light now so perhaps things will go quicker - it was certainly a dark night the last time.

There has been a good deal of fighting on our left the last few days and we have all sorts of news of gains and losses, but one has to wait for certain bits of news. The latest is that an advance has been made of a mile or two. Not our chaps but away on the left.

We have had flour issued today instead of bread so Jones got the folk here to find some yeast and they baked 90 big loaves, so that will help a good deal.

10.55 pm

As you see I am back in good time and things went A1 tonight so had no hanging about. I passed the 8th Transport a mile before the Dumping Ground waiting at their Rest Headquarters, so I got in before they did. None of the companies have arrived yet. They have to pass just at the top of the field.

The officers in the trenches were ordered to send their servants and kit out of the trenches as soon as it was dark, instead of waiting for the whole company. This saved my wagon two or three hours. The servants came in the wagons and will have the beds ready for the men.

Sunday 25th April 4.30 pm

We have had half a dozen of the officers in to enjoy hot baths today and they really enjoyed it. It's used up all our coals though so we'll have to scratch along for a day or two. We seem to have plenty of coke but tonight Jones and I will be off with a few fellows and a cart to search for wood. We will start after dark and see what we can find. I have had my eye on a broken-down farm near here for some time on the way to the trenches, so I expect to find what we need there.

There was a lot of loud firing last night and some today. Our trenches were heavily shelled yesterday but no one was hurt, although one or two had to be dugout. One fellow swore at his mate for throwing stones at him and then found it was a piece of shell.

Right - well - it looks like tea-time. One seems to be always eating in this place. Jones is having a rest so I shall wait until he's ready.

I would love you to see this room. There are pots and pans all about, water boiling on the range, raw meat ready for cooking. The table is neatly laid for two and I am writing at a table full of papers etc. There are big coats hanging about. It's quite a jumble sale show - but everything is clean and we are happy enough.

Monday 26th April 9.20 pm

The sleeping accommodation is good. A tiny room about 12 or 14 ft. square and just low enough for Jones, who is tall, to bash himself on the beams if he's not careful. He sleeps on the bed and I have a mattress on the floor. We both sleep in our valises.* There is a wash stand and a looking glass.

One of us gets out of bed first and gets dressed. This is usually Jones. Hill (my Orderly) washes my clothes here so I can get a change each week if I want it. It just depends if the spirit moves me or not!

Hill 60** is away on our left some way. You should see the huts near here where our fellows are now. The names! 'Rouster's Arms' 'The Hippodrome', 'Labour Bureau - Night Workers Wanted'.

How about the 'Bully Beef and Biscuit Inn'?

There is one fellow here, Jones Norton by name, who is quite a wit. He told us the other day that he had caught a water otter. When we went along to see it he'd a mess tin on a chain. They heat the water in their mess tins - hence water (h)otter!

Last night he went out to pinch wood for fires and found a dog kennel and brought it back and now the 'otter' lives in it. He also found an old sheepskin coat and made a cover for it.

We have had some fun as the Battalion Officers have been down in ones and twos and we have taken them all to see the 'otter'. One remarked before JN pulled it

* FOOTNOTE: *Kitbag cum sleeping bag*

** FOOTNOTE: *Hill 60, about three miles south-east of Ypres, is not a natural feature. It was made from the spoil removed during the construction of the railway line nearby. Because it was a small area of elevated land in a flat landscape, it had strategic importance in the battles in the Salient. It was the site of a famous battle in April 1915 on the Ypres Salient, and changed hands several times during the fighting. The remains of many soldiers from both the Allied and German forces still lie there. It is now maintained by the Commonwealth War Graves Commission. (note: interesting information about Hill 60 can be found on You Tube).*

'He told us the other day he had caught a water otter'
(Dog kennel for the water otter)

out that it was a shame to keep it in a kennel and we
ought to let it go. They've all been had by this. Captain
Lea and the Brigadier came to see it and fell for the trick
too. The Brigadier even said he would bring the Major
and the General to see it. Norton said he would go out
that day!

We have been felling trees and chopping wood this
afternoon. Coal has now become short. We brought a
ton back last night including a wheelbarrow and kennel
and a large chest for corn. We have had a flour delivery
again today so I have set one of my men, who is a baker
by trade, on the job. There are over a hundred loaves
here now and very splendid they look too.

Tuesday 27th April 6 pm

I thought I would just tell you what goes on while we are here. This is a wee rough sketch - not to scale. I shall not put in any roads.

The 7th go into the trenches tomorrow. They are at 'E' now, six miles back. Sunday night they will come out and go to farms at B & C, which is 2 miles back, and stay for four days. Then back to the trenches and the next time they come out they go to 'D' for four days. I am close to position 'D' at present.

I was going on a wood foraging tour night but my Sergeant wanted to go so he and Jones with 6 men have

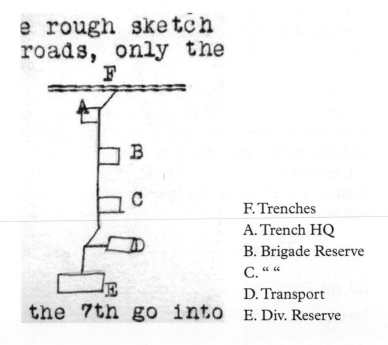

F. Trenches
A. Trench HQ
B. Brigade Reserve
C. " "
D. Transport
E. Div. Reserve

24

gone with a wagon. Its good fun as you are able to go to some ruined farm and search round for wood or anything else of use and as it's after dark no one can disturb you.

There are aircraft over us all day. One German dropped some stuff that affected the men's eyes and made them smart badly.*

Today I have had the field and all around the building here cleared up as there was a lot of rubbish that needed to be burned. It was rather lucky I had done it as the Adjutant came around after lunch. He told me that Brig. James puts us down as the smartest Battalion, so the Adjutant is very bucked having been complimented on the Brigade. So all's well for the present.

Our 'otter' has caused some fun again today!

The folk at this farm are topping. The old lady has a lovely face and can't do enough for us. She's always merry and bright and works very hard from 4.30 am until 6 or 7 pm.

Well - I shall have supper shortly. Boiled eggs and tea. Albert, our cook, is clearing the table so I shall have to close. He's an amusing fellow. I can't tell which eye he is looking at me with and he is always merry and bright too.

I am keeping in grand form and eating like a bull I must be eating heaps more than I do at home so I think you will find me fat and greasy when I return.

Thursday 29th April 6.15 pm

All the Battalions seem to report the same thing.

* FOOTNOTE: This must have been mustard gas

Fellows just missing shells and the dugouts getting knocked in. Men are also getting buried at times and they have to be dug out.

Friday 30th April 4 pm

Cyril was beside two men who have been blown to pieces. He escaped with a scratch on his left arm and a cut on his leg. He has had to go back to the hospital base while his leg gets better, which will be a week or two. He made 12 frs. As we had a bet as to who would get wounded first. I am writing home in case other reports get about. It shook Cyril up a lot.

There is a big show on to our left again today. They are shelling a place about to our left (Neuve Eglise) but I do not believe they have done much damage. The village is empty and has been rather to the fore in the papers lately. I see two Indians have got VC's for their work there.

I got well under fire last night. The Adjutant made us take some of the Company's food on three wagons further than we have been before and we were fired at. Half way there a party in front clearing a way for us came running along and fell behind the wagons and told us there was a machine gun trained on where they were working and they had been fired at three times. One cannot get horses to lie down and become invisible, so we did not go any further and unloaded where we were. Jones, a Sergeant and I followed the last wagon and had three shots aimed at us.

It is extraordinary how one ducks at the sound of a

bullet - you instinctively do it. We went to see the Adjutant and Jones told him it was no use going that way unless he wanted horses and drivers shot, so tonight we shall be on the Old Dump again.

The plan was to save the men 500-600 yards carrying rations but I do not see the advantage of exposing the animals like that.

Saturday 1st May 11.20 pm

Very quiet tonight. One of my drivers had a bullet through his cap - knocked it sideways - but the bullet missed him. He's quite delighted with the hole.

Our Battalion come out tomorrow.

I have no word of where Cyril has gone but perhaps I will have a line tomorrow. I have a parcel and a letter or two for him.

Monday 3rd May 12.15 noon

I did not write in the diary yesterday and left it until we returned. We were not back until 12.30 and it was 1 am before we ate. I saw Leslie last evening. He was quite fit. There's a rumour that F. Cooper has been killed but I am sure Leslie would have mentioned it if that were so. His chaps went back into the trenches again last night.

Let Bet's know I will get a photo of John Leslie Mellor* as soon as I get a camera and a chance. I usually see him during the daytime. Met him about 7 pm. last night and when they are in the huts here I can see him any time.

Today I seem to have slack morning. Two officers have just arrived - the first draft from the 2nd/7th. Greg Carr (Daddy as we used to call him) is one of them and a fellow called Pike. We also have a new interpreter - Belgian this time and a much better fellow in my opinion that the other. I am jolly glad the darned Frenchman is going - gives one the pip - such a worm.

There is great excitement out here now mouse hunting. I did wish I had 'Blobs' here yesterday - eight good rats in a cage, which is one night's haul. I am afraid to say there are any amount in this country.

That tall fellow - he's 6' 8" - from Caledon ('Baby' Lowe) has come to join the 6th Battalion. It's one officer for each Battalion.

During the last few days the crops are starting to get a move on. All the land is well cultivated here. It's about five or six months since the Germans were here. One of the grooms has gone sick and I will wait up for the ambulance.

Tuesday 4th May 7.29 pm

Up to now we have buried one man at the Trench Headquarters and I believe I told you he was my first reserve man for Transport.

We had the Germans here for a short time and I have a note for payment for dinner supplied to an Officer and 24 of his men.* The Germans though were in rather a hurry - both coming and going!

* FOOTNOTE: John Leslie Mellor was in the 6th Batt. RW Regt. He came from Lapworth, Warwickshire, and eventually became Major Hoskins' brother-in-law.

Albert is Captain Jones' man and does our cooking, as my man has the horse as well. Jones has a groom in addition. I really do most things myself and the Adjutant, wanting to make our fighting strength up, cut out as much as possible. It saves 2/6d a week.

9.40 pm: I have just finished supper and shall not be long before I go turn in. There have been a few shells I'm told dropped about a quarter of a mile from here. I think they are trying to find a big gun that has come up near here. They are a good way off and did no damage save turning up a little earth and I doubt they even killed a worm.

I went into the town Cyril went to and found that he went back from there on the 1st, so until he writes I will not know where he is and cannot send anything on to him - as letters only get sent back to base. You should just see my companions now - they are as happy and merry as could be. It's good to see them all fooling about.

Wednesday 5th May 9.5pm

I enjoyed a great game of football for an hour today with some of the men today and really enjoyed it.

I have been given a little more to do now as Brigade Transport Officer. I am to take over some work from Captain Lea so as to lighten his job. The trenches have to be kept in good repair all the time and to do so there

FOOTNOTE: This is clearly written in the diary, but it cannot be officially confirmed that such an event took place. Fraternisation with the enemy did not often take place. Nick Fear, an expert on the history of the Great War, believes this sounds like a journey to get a meal and supplies for a group at the front. It would have involved Captain Hoskins being shelled 'going in and out'. Supply lines were frequently a target.

are a thousand things to be sent there - wood, wire, sheets of iron, nails, sandbags. Each Battalion sends in a demand each day.

Captain Lea sends to the stores and draws as much as they can supply and gets it all to the Brigade HQ and we, according to who's in the trenches, take it up.

There is a lot of work attached, so Lea is handing it over to me. Also his transport wagons are most likely coming here as at present they are away from the Brigade HQ and he has no time to keep an eye on them.

I am to take over the ammunition supply to the Brigade and see the four Battalions are well supplied. Each Battalion has five small arms ammunition wagons. Three of these go to their Battalion and keep going backwards and forwards. Some are kept for emergencies. I am kept fed with stores by the Ammunition Co. while they in turn are fed by motorised lorries and so on right back. As the Battalions go forward I follow at a distance.

The remainder of my transport comes under my Sergeant and stands harnessed up ready to move at once upon receiving orders.

Heavy gunfire to our left has just started but up to this time it has been very still all day and now both sides are having a scrap for an area known as Famous Hill 60.

I am going to see the officer whom I will have to work with in the Ammunition supply column tomorrow or the next day.

Golly - there is a deuce of a show going on - something being lost or won at Hill 60. Those big guns go with such a deep boom-boom. Oh - I have just heard we have lost the Hill again.

Thursday 6th May 9.25 pm

Our Battalion go in tonight but I have been on Brigade jobs all day and did not get back until just now. I take over the stores for our Battalion tomorrow. The only part I do not like is that I shall have to get up an hour earlier so as to get to Brigade by 8 am.

Murray Junior is here. He's on a bomb throwing job tomorrow and he says he will be glad when it's over. I will make space for him to sleep on my mattress with me tonight.

Yesterday in one Regiment an officer and three men were killed at the 'game'. One of the places we have been in for a few days has been well shelled early today but I am glad to say they missed my provision shop.

Jones has gone up to the trenches and I hope he'll be back soon as I'm ready for supper.

Right - I have the letters to censor now and I hope there are not too many. I badly need a wash so perhaps I should get on with that first and then the censoring job.

Friday 7th May 9.10 pm

I have not been up to the trenches again tonight as I was on a Brigade job till nine and should still be there, only an order came through to cancel it all. I have been at Brigade nearly all day - anyone can have the job off me! There is no glory being there save the chance of getting jumped on. Still, since I happen to be Transport Officer for Brigade I will give it my best I do not care what they give me to do in any department. I will just do my best and they will have to be satisfied or get someone else. I have always got on well with Captain Lea and the 7th happens to be in his good books just now.

Things are very still tonight. They have been still all day except for a few shells. They were after our artillery - and missed I'm told!

Saturday 8th May 5.50 pm

So Cyril is at home. I hope he is about right again. He said nothing about his leg in his letter.

We get heaps of daily papers. I have been on Brigade jobs most of the day. My sergeant will have to do more - he has to take charge should an advance take place any time.

It is not so hot today as there is a strong wind blowing but it is warm enough to make one slack.

Saw Les today - he said he had been down here last evening to see me and in fact had tea here but I was out and Jones forgot to mention it to me. I promised to go and have tea at his hut today but unfortunately I did not get there. Leslie looks A1. If there is not much to do tomorrow I will pop up and have a chat with him.

10.30 pm: I have to report to Brigade HQ at 4 am tomorrow morning so I had better be off to bed. I have just got in from trench HQ.

Sunday 9th May 2.50 pm

It is a quiet Sunday here today. I left the farm at 3.45 this morning and reached here at 4 am and I suppose here I shall most likely remain until tomorrow. Captain Lea is here too but the General and Major Higginson are out.

I had a couple of hours' sleep between five and seven, breakfast at eight, arranged for today's stores and read 'Punch' and other papers etc. There's a note here re: transport. It says I have too many men. I say NOT SO. We shall see tonight.

I guess Cyril is having a good time today. I can just picture him if Leslie gets home.

I may not get your letter today unless my Sergeant brings it when he comes to draw stores about six or seven.

I am seated in an armchair of sorts - quite comfy but not strong! The sun is keeping me warm but there is a very keen wind. Hallo! Lea is showing signs of forty winks - I must say I could do with the same.

Sitting here taking things easy is something like Sunday - except of course for the bloody guns, which keep cracking all the time. There appears to be a bit of a show on today as a matter of fact.

Monday 10th May 7.35

Got back to camp at 11.30 pm and am now off to Brigade again. Looks like a topping day.

We are all hoping to have Col. Elton back as he's such a fine man, but I am afraid we shall not get him. No one has been put in his place yet. Major Knox is the commanding officer at present. Major Hake is the Junior.

There were a few men killed yesterday - three killed and nine wounded. The 5th had six killed and fifteen wounded. There was a bit of a show on to keep the Germans occupied all along the Line while the French gave a push lower down, as doubtless you will see in the papers in due course.

I was at Brigade HQ all day so as to be ready to run more ammunition up if required.

So our full total killed is now five - and I don't know how many wounded - two dozen or so I would say and then one must not forget the sick and the sprained limbs.

Leslie asked me if I'd received my cake. I am going to his hut for breakfast tomorrow as he has a PORK PIE! I shall get there about 9.30 after I've been to the Brigade.

The battle of Hill 60 is not finished - it will be ours when it is.

Tuesday 11th May

Had Leslie and Brian to lunch which also enabled them to enjoy a hot bath.

Wednesday 12th May 4.20 pm

I have been altering some head stalls all day. The sergeant and I are getting jolly good at saddler's work. The sergeant takes charge when I am away. I am still of course responsible but do more supervising and less donkey work. Tea is ready and then I must off to Brigade.

I have to fetch the Battalion out of the trenches. They have been in six days this time.

Ah - the new Colonel has arrived - named Price. I am told he is considered to be a very good man. He came and had a look at the horses today and is quite satisfied.

He said we had a jolly good stamp.

Thank goodness we are not for the trenches tonight as it has been raining all day and would be very unpleasant. The mud is awful with the smallest shower so you can guess a day's rain makes things very sloppy.

There is heavy firing to the right of us. The French are pushing forward.

I have had eight or nine officers today for hot baths and some stayed to lunch and tea so have had quite a reception.

I am getting wood tomorrow to building a shelter to enable rations to be dished out here and to keep the meat under. In the warmer weather Jones and I will feed under there also.

I will get the wood tomorrow when ordering the wood for the trenches. I had better order extra and send one of my wagons to draw it straight from here instead of going to the Brigade.

I have mentioned this to Captain Lea just to be on the safe side and he said it would all right but keep quiet about it! I will enjoy knocking the place together. I will get some wood also for the adjutant as he wants some for the huts.

I am going to get another riding horse for myself so now I have managed to get two extra horses - or rather mules. I must say I do not see why I should not have another gee and have one spare. I do more riding than anyone else and it's really too much for one horse to keep up to scratch. I am six light draught short so I am hoping to get a suitable one of those. If not, next time I send a return in I will make it so many Light Draught and one riding horse Officer's Charger - and see what I get. There are always ways and means of working these things when one knows the ropes.

I need a horse a shade bigger than Dick but the same stamp. Dick's a topper and keeps fit. We are great pals.

Ah - I hear we are now the 48th Division and the 143rd Brigade. This has only just come out . We have not known who we were before:

So 1/7 Royal Warwickshire Regiment,
143 Brigade
48 Division
Ex: Force T.

So note the address you can use now. Let the folk know at home will you?

All the Battalions are being numbered and it will make it much easier.

I have the wood for the shed cover I mentioned yesterday and also nails, so I shall make a start tomorrow and hope for fine weather.

Saturday 15th May

Here is the plan of just the farm. The bathroom is a wee place where two fellows sleep and we take in a tub - a good wide one - to sit in. All the floors are paved eight-inch square tiles, black and white as a rule.

Upstairs is one big room used for storing straw etc. and it has an entrance from outside. That is where the

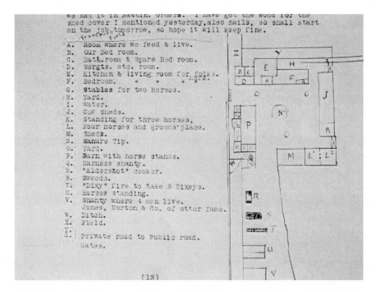

we had it in battin, order. I have got the wood for the
shed cover I mentioned yesterday, also nails, so shall start
on the job tomorrow, so hope it will keep fine.

A. Room where we feed & live.
B. Our Bed room.
C. Bath room & Spare Bed room.
D. Sergts. etc. room.
E. Kitchen & living room for folks.
F. Bedroom.   "   "   "   "
G. Stables for two horses.
H. Yard.
I. Water.
J. Cow Sheds.
K. Standing for three horses.
L. Four horses and grooms' place.
M. Sheds.
N. Manure Tip.
O. Yard.
P. Barn with horse stands.
Q. Harness shanty.
R. "Aldershot" cooker.
S. Sweeds.
T. "Dixy" fire to take 5 Dixeys.
U. Horses standing.
V. Shanty where 4 men live.
   Jones, Norton & Co, of other fame.
W. Ditch.
X. Field.
Y.
Z. Private road to Public road.
   Gates.

(13)

men hang out - at least all those who have not made
shanties in the field.

The 'Aldershot' stove you may know is made of clay.
One burns wood in the hole and get the whole thing
hot, then clear out the fire and put the meat in where it
roasts. You want the sides of the stove thick so that it
holds the heat.

The other is special and saves fuel. The ground is cut
out about eighteen inches deep and twelve inches wide,
then a piece of iron is laid on the top, cut out thus for the
'dixeys' to rest in, leaving space for the fire to burn below.
We make a chimney from a biscuit box to finish it off.
Quite a small fire keeps them boiling as no heat is lost
and the sides and bottom get backed and hold the heat.

The Colonel has been down today and is quite pleased
with the horses and everything. All that he could find

was that I should have the manure sprinkled with paraffin to kill the flies.

I have been given the grooms' and officers' horses under my special care as the new Colonel thinks it should be so. He also wants the grooms to be used for any jobs that may crop up. The previous adjutant would not allow them to do very much, which made them feel like real fools.

You can probably tell I like the new Colonel. He's really up to date and has got one or two things done that I could not get permission for before.

We shall not move from this area for some time. Both flanks must get ahead well first. We may at any time be moved somewhere else and someone else of course placed here but that is not seeming likely at this time.

A strange thing happened to my groom today. He accompanied me to the Brigade. We were there by 8 am. When we came back I rode up our field to talk to the Brigade Cpl. My groom felt something at the back of his neck and - guess what - he pulled a little mouse out! It must have been on him for about two hours. He said he thought he had heard quaint noises somewhere near!

I have to keep an eye on the Brigade HQ horses up at their farm. I had a look around today and had to tell off one of the General's grooms. If any of my men had their officer's horses in the state they were in I should send him back to the Battalion.

An officer's groom is a soft job - the softest thing going and 2/6d. a week extra - so a man's a fool to lose the job.

Tuesday 18th May, 8.45 pm

I saw Leslie yesterday evening for a few minutes. He was having a good go in at all the goods you'd sent him from home. He gave me one of Bet's apples. I had supper with him and jolly good it was too. I have promised to go for lunch today but was not eventually able to get there.

I was up at 7 am and went to Brigade, leaving about 9.30 having seen to the Stores and also had a look at the yard and shed where the stores are kept to get it straight and to my liking. Had a good look at the horses and arranged for some ammunition to be fetched.

I had to stir up the General's groom yesterday as he had not been looking after the horses at all - in fact they were beastly dirty. I shall get him moved if he does not keep them spotless now. The Junior Captain's horse is looked after better.

I think the grooms at the Brigade were rather taken aback at being cussed at by me and had heaps of excuses, all of which I have heard before, so they did not get much change.

I got back here abut ten and after having a look at my own gees I made a table for my men to feed on in their place. Up to now they have used the floor. That took me up to lunchtime and afterwards I had the letters to censor.

Then I got several little things done and also went around the lines, which can take me either ten minutes or several hours.

4.30 pm came in no time. At five I left for the Brigade to see what RE Stores had arrived and arrange for its disposal to the trenches, cast an eye over the horses there and got back here abut 6.30. I had a job to do on the horse lines and was late for supper.

There is always something to on my job.

It has rained here nearly all day and all yesterday so there is mud everywhere and such sticky mud too.

The news all round is good. The French and the Belgians are both pushing ahead. I am told some of the German prisoners are reported to have given themselves up in large numbers. They have said they are sick of it all and - like us - wish to goodness it was all over.

'My groom felt something at the back of his neck.......'

Friday 21st May, 8.50 pm

Col. Price is A1 but unfortunately we may lose him. There was some muddle and he was not supposed to be with us. Someone else should be here! I do so hope he does not leave. He was round the lines today and was very pleased.

The guns are booming away to our right, a very heavy bombardment is taking place. Judging from last time we heard it over there, it is along that piece of line we pushed forward a week or so ago. The sound is very much as you would hear it in a large town, when in a room with windows closed while any amount of traffic is passing.

I have been working all day. I was out at Brigade then the Stores, then to the 1/8th . This afternoon I have been getting the horse stands rearranged and the ground bricked over. I was without tie or collar with my sleeves rolled up shovelling earth when the Colonel and Colonel Stewart with Major Knox arrived. I was so busy I did not notice them until the Colonel spoke.

I draw my six light draught horses tomorrow. You should just see my horses now - they look lovely and all as fit as one could wish - their new coats beginning to look well.

The Colonel remarked he could almost see his face in them when he viewed the riding horses. He's quite pleased with his own groom. I think he'll do but shall be able to tell better in a week's time.

Saturday 22nd May, 12 noon

Ye gods - it's hot today!

I am waiting for those remounts to come. They did not arrive last evening so I had to send again today at 8 am I gave Morgan the job as last time he made rude remarks. He will be delighted at being kept hanging about waiting all morning.

A bomb exploded in one of my wagons a day or two ago. I had to bring eleven boxes of jam pot bombs to the Brigade HQ from our Trench HQ. Jam pot bombs are old jam pots filled with various things; they make good bombs.

Just before reaching the first farm the blessed bomb went off, making a deuce of a row and flash. It blew off the driver's cap and really set the gees off at a gallop. The horses were pulled up just by the farm and they waited for me to come. I soon had the bally ten boxes out and into a field. Luckily the thing did not do too much damage or we would have had a wagon smashed up. No damage was done except to the driver's cap which was muddy and wet.

It was a new pattern jam pot which has a special switch one has to twist which lights the fuse. They are dangerous items, these bombs. One gets all sorts and types. The last few patterns are topping and as safe as a house when carefully handled.

We have a new Colonel arrived so now we have two at present and shall not know for a day or two which one is to stay.

Oh - it will be no use Cyril bringing a camera out as another order has been received for all to be collected again.

Those horses are darned late - its nearly 12.30 and they should have been here by 9.30. One can never tell when a remount train will come to a day or so.

I plan a joy-ride with Auster of the 8th Battalion Transport to see some of the Div. T. Officers we were with at Chelmsford. We start at 2.30.

Replica Jam Pot Bomb to be found at the Royal Warwickshire Regt. Museum

Sunday 23rd May 2.45 pm

The new Colonel is expected to come and have a look around shortly. The six new horses I had yesterday are topping. They arrived at last. Real good animals of a good size and all black. I have only two poor-looking animals now out of 77. One of the new ones may make a good mount but I am not very keen about him. Also it would cut up the pairs to take him away.

Some shelling last night and early this morning and also a few shells dropped near our Battalion. The Adjutant's groom was up there when two came and he saw them burst very near. Then on his way back he had one in front of him. He does not know if anyone was hurt. He's always saying 'Damn the shells'.

At about 8 am a powder magazine near here exploded and killed eight men. I suspect one of them was smoking in there.

Our man are back to the trenches tomorrow night and it seems no time since they were coming out. How time does fly.

We have a wee dog now - a topping terrier fellow. He followed a man who came from a town near by and we kept him. He's quite at home and has been made a member of the 'Black Hand Band' who are some of the fellows who live in a shanty on the field.

Had a sumptuous meal last night. I went to supper at Morgan's place and Durham Elkington was there. He's a great gourmet. Supper began with a savoury, whites of egg filled with something delicious, then we had soup, chicken, stewed cherries and sardines on toast. All this followed by coffee, whisky and soda, cigars etc. We drank beer during the meal.

Beer is like champagne at home for price, more or less!

Anyway, I was well filled when I came away. Oh - I have forgotten the dessert, and there was also a salad.

Durham got into his pyjamas as we were leaving at 10 pm. Beautiful yellow silk ones with navy blue collar and cuffs. I told him if he put on a wig of lovely long hair he'd not look so bad!

Jolly quaint coming back as guns and rifle fire could be easily heard and any amount of flashes over by the trenches. Just the night for a garden dance.

I have not heard anything of how the 6th are getting on. Leslie comes to the huts on Tuesday. I guess he and Rabone will be here for a bath and a cuppa.

The Colonel is late - perhaps he's not coming.

Captain Hanson's servant was shot in the foot last time they were in and his brother - a sergeant - was killed.

We have had much better luck than the 8th.

Tuesday 25th May 4 pm

Here is a copy of a letter from Col. Elton and may be of interest to you. You see he was rather proud of the Battalion he commanded for a few months. I hope Col. Price is going to stay with us. He's a topper and a sound man.

We took the Battalion into the trenches last night and a very light night too. We could not go over the hill before 9 pm.

Special Order 23rd May, 1915:

The following Special Order is published for the information of all officers, NCOs and men of the Battalion at the request of Colonel Elton:

'As I have been obliged to relinquish the command of the Regiment, owing to severe illness, I am anxious that the Officers, NCOs and men of the Battalion should know how deeply I regret having to depart from the Regiment at such a time and how much I feel not being able to be with them at the Front.

I consider any officer who has the honour to command the 1/7th Royal Warwickshire Regiment is very much to be congratulated.

I know well how the officers have striven to support me under all circumstances and how splendidly the NCOs and men have behaved under very trying conditions - a combination of effort and spirit 'de corps' that cannot fail to make a Regiment equal to going anywhere and doing anything. I have always had this feeling about the 1/7th and my regret is more than I can say that I am perforce unable to be with you - and if necessary to have died with you.

In saying good-bye to you all I wish you every luck possible and may you rest assured I shall never forget you. I hope you all know that I consider it a very great honour to have commanded you.

A. G. G. Elton, Lieut. Colonel.

Thursday 27th May 2.20 pm

Quite a nice still night up at HQ last evening. Col. Price is very popular. He was going round the trenches a day or two back and noticed one Dugout was very dirty; also it was named the 'Rosary', so he called for the owners and told them they had better put up a new place calling it 'Pigsty'. As you can guess - it was soon cleaned.

I saw Leslie this morning. Their new Colonel seems to be giving them a great amount of extra parades. He's new to the job and rather too pushing for out here. The fellows want rest when up at the Huts of course.

Friday 28th May 2.35 pm

There was another big explosion near here yesterday at one of the bomb making places. Twelve killed and I do not know how many wounded. A Colonel who was passing at the time with his orderly on horseback was were blown to pieces. Both horses killed but the orderly was not even hurt.

I am told six officers were also killed in the explosion. Also last night about eight were killed while trying to find guns. The Germans dropped a few shells by the 5th Dump and farms the men were in. Three fell on part of the road we pass, but as it happened we were ten minutes behind them.

I have put up three fly-papers since lunch and two are nearly full already. They seem very popular. These flies really get annoying.

Try and get 'Punch' of the 19th May and read 'Watch-

Dogs'. It is written by a man in the trenches next to us on the left. In the issue of the 19th he mentions a handcart - that is in front of our left trenches. It is all fact and quite amusing.

Our medicine case came in useful again yesterday. One of my fellows has a rotten head. I gave him an 'sq'* and he felt much better at once and quite well in an hour or so. My fellows have perfect faith in it now.

10.50 pm: I am just back from the trenches. Topping night. Trench HQ had been shelled about an hour before we went down there. Our fellows had cleared out into their dugouts, placed near for that purpose.

I've had a full day - I was at Brigade at 7.30 and have been on the go most of the time since.

Stevens, the QM of the 1/1st RAMC Howkins gang, came in. Howkins is known as 'Puff' and it is rather a neat name for him.

Jones is up at the Hutments waiting or the Battalion to come in. One company went by just as I came back. The 8th were late relieving. I passed them on the hill and had most of my wagons away before they came.

Eveson came down to see me between 5 and 6.30. I am sorry I was away at the Brigade.

* *Further explanation of this item has not been found.*

Saturday 29th May 3.45 pm

Really, one does not want for much out here, which you will find surprising I know. Jones makes various dishes out of ration food, which makes a change and keeps us going. I'm as fit as possible and going strong.

Sunday 30th May 9 pm

Today when walking to the Brigade after tea I saw a big cloud of smoke coming from the same place as the first time and hear that they were loading some powder boxes on to a wagon when they exploded, smashing the wagon, killing the horses. The driver got away with a broken leg.

We drew 500 today and luckily no trouble up to date. The Sergeant saw something smoking on a wagon and had it thrown quickly off. It exploded without damaging anyone or anything.

I have not seen the horsefly nets out here yet. They are not troubled at present but no doubt will be later.

I am very sorry to report that Col. Price went today to rejoin his old Battalion. It does seem rot - here we have a man set out from home who knows nothing of this darned war - only joined the war started and there is Price who has been out all the time and a Regular well able to command a Battalion and he has to go back to take over a Company. He's a Colonel at that! Fancy making him do Company work when he'd make a real sound Battalion Officer.

I had a spill today but not hurt. I was on the way to Brigade this morning at 8.15. I was late and just along from here before I reached the road old Dick stumbled badly and went down flop. I turned a complete somersault over his head! He was up first of course and just turned on to some grass to graze while I picked myself up and go dusted down. Glad to say old Dick is none the worse.

Monday 31st May 4.15 pm

There is only one bomb I like. That is a Topper, quite a gentleman's bomb! It is called the 'Lemon Bomb' and is just the shape and size of a large lemon. There is little or no chance of it doing anything silly and it's a beauty on its job. Made in Birmingham! Only a few arrived yet.

A replica lemon bomb (Royal Warwickshire Regt. Museum)

There are hundreds of various kinds. Why they do not make half a dozen patterns and get a good supply I don't know.

I have made a new washing stand for my men today – it's just a stand for the basins, made of various tins.

They empty the water down the centre and it runs off into a brook. Also I have had a big hole dug beside the brook 4' 6" deep and bricked on the bottom. The flow of the brook keeps it clean - and makes a topping place for a cold bath.

I had a hot bath today by the way. The Brigadier was around my lines last night while I was at the Brigade and was pleased so he said. He said the condition of the horses was wonderful. One up to me!

Morgan has his good too. He runs us very close - the 5th and 8th haven't a look in. The 5th is the worse. I will have to buck them up but its not an easy job when you are a transport of your own in the same Brigade.

Our chaps go back into the trenches tomorrow night and the 8th comes up to the huts so I'll be seeing Leslie during the next day or two. He will be up at Brigade Reserve Farms.

Tuesday 1st June 2.40 pm

Major Knox was hit by a piece of shell in the shoulder. It only bruised him. He did not have to leave and kept on with his duties.

We have some of K's men in the trenches, to learn things. There are many of them all about the place. Lots of troops and guns playing around.

Wednesday 2nd June 3 pm

It's no use grousing on this show. Take what comes and make the best of it. Perhaps when we begin to move I'll start to get ruffled. That, I am told, is the Big Test.

I have just been out to have a look around as I'd told my Sergeant to put some horses in a different place, away from the barn where they get too hot and also knock pieces of skin off at night by going to sleep standing up and falling down. I am putting them under some trees on grass.

Thursday 3rd June

No Warwicks were hurt in any of the explosions, although some of our wagons drew powder boxes the morning of the accident. We are having very few casualties. Other Battalions are suffering more. The 5th and 8th seem to get it worse as a rule.

Two officers in the former have been killed - one last night and one today; both shot in the head when looking over the parapet. One was Johnnie Francis and the other Edgerton from Edgbaston. Francis was very popular with the other men and both are a big loss to the Brigade. A big shock to us all, being the first officers and their deaths so close together. We are all rather down.

Saturday 5th June, 6pm

I have just returned from HQ and have been watching the Germans shell some farm buildings. No military people are there and they set two on fire. It seems to amuse them to shell these places - or it may be the road nearby they are ranging in on.

Our men come out of the trenches tonight. They have had a quiet time for once.

I have had a harness and wagon inspection today by Major Goode. One would think we were getting ready for a Regimental Display and Show the way one is told keep the tackle clean. Mind you I like to see it smart when possible and it does look well.

Keay of 1/5th took a toss off his horse and got dragged 50 yds or so, getting a sprained ankle, cut face and slight concussion, so he'll be away for a month or more

Monday 7th June, 2.5 pm

I have been on Brigade jobs all morning and have to get a move on again at 2.30 pm. There are a pile of letters to sign also.

We are going to change over with one of the other Battalions soon. I believe we have to change and change about for the purpose of keeping mobile and it means everyone knows the whole of our Divisional line then.

It will be a bally nuisance to have to quit this place. We have shaken down so well and I quite expected to stay here until we pushed forward. We are quite mobile and in good repair for a move unless the horses are too fat.

I am giving my gee a rest for a week or two. I've ridden him hard ever since we came here without his being any the worse for it, but I do not like to wear out a willing mount.

Tuesday 8th June, 3.20 pm

There is a thunderstorm knocking around here today. Started about 2 pm. We only had a touch of it - it is very hot and humid and I hardly slept last night for the heat.

I had a full day yesterday. In the saddle up to 7 pm nearly all the time after various stores in the timber line chiefly.

At 7 pm I was up with our Battalion, which has

moved into some huts under the hill, and soon found a few jobs to do and am now ready for a bite of supper.

Our new Division General is stirring us up a good deal and the Brigadier is poking his nose about. Just now his speciality is Transport. We are to do more drill and rifle exercises etc. The Transport men look like having a busy time soon. The Brigadier has got an idea that because they do not go in the trenches they should do twice the work the other men do! He will forget about it in a week or two.

I have been asking Col. Harris, boss of the whole Division, if there were any respirators for horses. He tells me that it has been discovered in affected areas that the horses are not affected. Umm.

Thursday 10th June 4 pm

We are nine officers short at present, one way or another. Both the last draft officers have gone away sick. Major Hale is the only one away wounded but he is not at all likely to return as they say he'll not regain the use of his hand.

Friday 11th June 2.20 pm

We have moved to our right. The new General plans to keep the Battalions and Brigades moving around so that every four or eight days we move and everybody will know the trenches.

I did not get to bed until 2.30 this morning. Our Battalion came out of the trenches - likewise the 5th and

8th. The 6th moved out of ours and into some more. The fellows we take over from here have only had about two men killed up to now, so they will find our trenches a little more exciting.

This billet is A1 - a bedroom all to myself. We feed in style, waited upon by an aged handmaiden who - by the way - has a very pretty daughter of about 19! It is a private house - not a farm. The Transport are about ¼ mile away.

I have been making tables and washing stands for the men today. The men are all under wagon sails etc. as the barn place for them is rotten. Water here is not plentiful as it was at our last place.

This is a most enjoyable billet. Here I am in a topping room and bed with clean sheets and as happy as a lark. I can hear rifle fire plainly, although we must be three miles back from the line - perhaps two. As the Battalion are resting I am not going to do more than necessary.

Sunday 13th June 10 pm

I had to be on the lines at 3 pm to take a batch of reserve transport men to riding school. I have ten of them for seven days. I am giving them one hour morning and afternoon apart from the ordinary routine of stables etc.

I had the first hours drill for all men and NCOs at my lines, which includes the Quarter Master's men and post men etc. I am ordered to do so daily so as to keep them up to scratch. The idea is good really - it is to keep them ready so that should the Bosh suddenly break through along our line and no time to get the transport and stores away we can take up our merry men (four transports would mean 200 men). They would get in some position and open fire on the approaching Germans, which would give our men time to rally and for the supports to come up.

The Bosh would be surprised at the sudden blow and thinking reserves were there, hold up a jiff and just that check might mean saving a nasty situation.

My men are a jolly gang - all young save one or two and as willing as one could wish.

Monday 14th June 10.15 pm

We were turned out of bed at 5 am today. At least Jones and I were. We should have received a note at 3 am but I am pleased to say the messenger could not find us. The 3 am message was to 'Stand by' and the 5 am warning where to meet the Battalion. As a matter of fact that place was just outside here. On waking, instead of having the wagons and pack ready to join the Battalion I was in bed and quite happy.

Anyway I got a move on as soon as I got it into my head that something was up and had some wagons up in 50 minutes from receiving the order in bed.

Its all settled down nicely and we went home for breakfast. A mine had been exploded under one of our trenches and caused the 'Stand-to'.

Tuesday 15th June 9.30 pm

We have moved again back behind our old place. The

5th and 7th are in the trenches with 6th and 8th in reserve. We were inspected yesterday by our new Divisional General Fanshaw.

Wednesday 16th June 9.45 pm

I have plenty of work to do nowadays. The Brigade Transport are with me again and also the Signal section wagons etc. The Brigade are some way off and I have a phone with four operators here, so I have to see to Trench stores on my own.

My ten men on a Ride & Drive Course are doing well. I had them out with two horses and wagon today and they did quite well.

Morgan has been in for supper and says his ten chaps have not been on a horse yet. He's too busy to see to them (so he says!).

Today I was up at 6 and out at 6.30. Breakfast was at 8 and I was on the lines until 10 when the indent for trench stores arrived.

On the lines again at 11.

Got back at 4 pm and dished out trench stores and watched the Ride & Drive men driving with the wagons. After tea I checked all the transport farms to make sure all was well.

Thursday 17th June 9.10 pm

I went to Brigade HQ after lunch and just after my man and I passed through a village nearby it was shelled. The enemy dropped about a dozen in. It is the first time I have been shelled. When we came back we saw several holes in the road and one went plump into the church, which has been knocked about badly. Folk are living still in the village, although it gets shelled most days.

There is a rumour about that we were to go back to Blighty on the 22nd of this month and could stay three weeks and then go to India to relieve some Regulars. That tale will not come off I assure you!

Friday 18th June 9 pm

An amusing incident occurred a few days ago. Some of K's army were passing our lines (on a route march for health!). My fellows were close by watching them pass and I heard one of my men ask one of them 'Which advertisement fetched you here Bill?'. Nasty. I have also heard them called 'Advertisement Answers'.

They are mostly big, fine fellows and should do well.

We keep getting officers and a few men for instruction. A Quartermaster and Transport Officer belonging to K's Suffolk Regiment came today. We give them all the information we can. The chief thing they want to know is how the food is taken up. Our Quartermaster gets the strength of men in trenches per Company and divides the rations to that. If 'A' Company has four trenches then the rations are divided into four parts, in equal percentage of men in each trench, and sends it on in a wagon marked 'A'. Very simple.

Some send rations up and the Company Quartermaster Sergeant has to do the dividing.

I was on the field today watching the Ride and Drive class. I'd got them on horses with wagons, so I put up some pegs for them to drive through. At one place they all went wide or knocked the pegs down, so I had a shot and found it was really tricky.

I offered 2 frs to anyone who could get through clean and they could try as often as they liked, also with their own pairs. One did it after six shots - and then another who had been out returned and did it first time. One of the Ride and Drive class managed it and then one other managed it after several shots. It was quite a bit of fun for 40 minutes.

Tomorrow we are having a match against the 8th, who are at the same game - they are in the next field. It all helps to give the men practice and more control of their horses.

I am now buying my men 4d. worth of milk a day to go in their morning tea. It is not a 'ration' as you can perhaps understand. The milk is just enough to take the sharpness from plain tea.

Saturday 19th June 2.30 pm

Some news! Two of our officers and six men are off today for five or seven days' leave. That number are to go each week apparently. They should get three days and four nights at home. One officer is here now. He came in for lunch and I have packed him off to bed for an hour.

My turn should come round. Let's see - 28 officers - 14 weeks - I am sure to be the last, as those who have been in the trenches will come first. (Those poor chaps have had more nervous strain than us luckier ones at the rear.) That means two and a half months to my turn. I may have a chance at the beginning of August then.

Umm - taking the men at six a week, it will take about 2½ years to get through the Battalion, so those who get leave will be lucky.

There's a joke out here about how long one thinks the war is going to last. The reply is 'Well - I hardly know but I am told the first seven years will be strenuous, the next three not so bad and after that one will be used to it'.

I believe we shall see some fighting soon. There is a feeling that something may happen at any moment.

Our Battalion are supposed to be coming out of the trenches again tonight but there is an order to stand by, so they may not be relieved. I am awaiting further instructions.

Sunday 20th June 3.45 pm

My Ride and Drive competition went well - that is to say, my men won, but not as easily as I would have wished.

First we had single pairs in limbered wagons round a circle and driving through four sets of blocks. Then at a trot, followed by 2 pairs in each, walk and trot. Then we put the lead horses in as wheelers and did the same. Then we had four sets of blocks in a straight line and took the wagons through - one on top of the other with four teams in and counted the blocks knocked down.

The blocks were out six inches wider than the width of the wheels. The winners of the competition were to take 10 frs. If the 1/8th won, I paid. If we won Auster paid. The whole event took a couple of hours to get through and created much excitement.

Tuesday 22nd June

A note appeared in orders yesterday reading thus:

> *'Censorship': The following order is published for information and strict compliance. The following subjects are being frequently mentioned in private correspondence. Hours, dates and system of relief, position of batteries and observing stations, railway construction, mining and bridging operations, supply of ammunition, position and description of billets, situation of HQ's of Divisional Brigades etc. Casualties (generally very exaggerated), criticisms of other branches of allied troops and superiors.*
>
> *All these items are covered by the Prohibitions in Censor Regulations but the fact in all cases does not appeared to be realised.'*

So again, we are warned to be careful. It does not affect anything I have told you up to now.

Wednesday 23rd June 11.15 am

I have had the Brigade Transport Officers in today to explain a few things to them. I like them to get together now and again. I've a little exciting news today.

I went along with those wagons last evening and on reaching the point where the turn is. From the main road to Brigade HQ is about 500 yards along. I sent my mounted Orderly to tell the Corporal to send the wagons along singly a hundred yards apart, and two turned down the drive.

The drive, as I say, is 500 yards long, with a deep ditch on the left for 250 yards. Then a drive crosses it on the right and there is a small ditch and some crops. After the bridge is a high hedge on the left and the deep ditch on the right. At the top there is a dead-end save for a gateway into a field.

'The horses, apparently driverless, were coming at me full gallop'

I turned off the main road and it was dark by then, being a dull evening with rain threatening. A wagon with two horses followed behind. Before they were off the main road I heard the driver yell for them to stop and on looking round could not see him. Had he fallen off? He was still shouting and the horses began to gallop.

The horses - apparently driverless - were coming at me full gallop. I saw the only thing to do was to get on ahead and give them time to stop - so away I went on Old Dick.

The horses gained on me and I tried to pull Dick into the crops, but in the dark he wouldn't go. The wagon and horses were following close behind and no driver to be seen. So we arrived at the bend.

I decided in two ticks to keep to the drive and took the bend in grand style, expecting the horses and wagon to go straight on and pull up alongside me, which would have given me the chance to grab a rein. On glancing behind though I was blowed to see they followed me and cleared the bend and were coming for me at the deuce of a pace. Off I went again harder than ever.

Some men were coming towards us so I shouted to them to clear out of the way, which they did pretty sharpish.

The horses had by now pulled up to within a couple of yards of me, all going like bats out of hell.

The next question was what was to happen at the end, for I had only been up there once and could not remember anything but a dead end. I remember thinking that it would not be long before I was in hospital as I could picture my horse and me getting bowled over and trampled on and dragging myself from under a pile of horses and wagons all smashed up together. Really quite thrilling!

I galloped full tilt up to the end of the drive, the horses close on my gee's heels. At the end there is a gateway into a field sharp left, so I pulled Old Dick through there and waited for the wagon to smash past, but - no - they darned well followed me again and came to a halt 50 yards past me in front of some barbed wire.

I jumped down and giving Dick to someone to hold, ordered an ambulance man to go and attend to the Driver who was not with the wagon.

Both horses and wagon were untouched and not damaged. The driver only had his knees grazed slightly.

Apparently the driver had got bumped clean off his seat in the wagon on to one of the horses and then fell between the two, holding on to the pole and one trace, but finding that uncomfortable he decided he'd do better to let go, which he did and the wheels passed each of him and missed him altogether, leaving me with the two horses chasing after me alone.

Anyway, all turned out well and I sent the man off to have a wash and be attended to. I then went to report that I had arrived. I saluted the General, Brigade Major and Captain, saying 'I've arrived sir, at the double!'

'So it seems, Hoskins' they replied.

It had struck me as I was galloping along that it was a complete nightmare in reality, but at the same time I could not help noticing how wonderful those two horses appeared chasing along madly not two yards behind me. It probably only lasted a couple of minutes.

We move again shortly. The whole Division goes back I believe. Cannot give details of course as orders are not out.

Thursday 24th June 9.10 pm

There is a troop of men passing singing 'Who's your lady friend'. They sound happy and there are two or three mouth organs accompanying.

We will be on the same game tomorrow night back to the place we've been to twice before - just for the night and a day then back further - where to or for how long one never knows.

All leave has been stopped for a time so I don't expect to be home for some time.

Oh - I've just heard that the man whose horses bolted a day or two ago has been hit by shrapnel when taking trench stores up tonight. I do not know if this is right and have sent to make sure.

One fellow had his ear nearly bitten off by a horse today and another man has been kicked, causing a deep cut in his leg. A third has gone sick so they are all gone away to hospital..

Friday 25th June 3 pm

There is a strange mixture of guns and thunder today - which is guns and which is thunder? - and here comes the rain.

Tuesday 29th June 11.45 am

We have been on the move, so there has been no post in or out. I hear there are 240 bags of mail for the Brigade, so it will take some time to sort out. We are to be here for about seven days, all being well. Our last four nights have been on the march.

Wednesday 30th June 7.10 pm

This is a topping wee place and we are all quite comfy. The men are in decent barns and places. The horses are A1 and all going well.

There goes my shoeing smith and his mate. They have just been repairing some of the brakes. The brakes on these wagons are poor and need constant attention.

The new travelling kitchens are all breaking up now. The 8th have three gone, the 5th one and the 6th two. Ours have remained intact but no doubt they will follow. The axles break - made in too much of a hurry and not nearly strong enough.

Leave is to be ON again and is to be seven days instead of five.

We had a very interesting lecture today by our new Brigade Major, all about how an attack is carried out.

Friday 2nd July

I should not be surprised if we get a Test Alarm tonight as I believe we are to have one some time soon.

I'm off to my lines now and hear a General of some kind may be about. I will not be straightening things up. I always make the boast that anyone can come and inspect my lines at any time and have mighty little to grouse about. When I have an inspection by outsiders I never do extra work and I've not let myself down yet. I am very proud of my Transport, more so than it merits perhaps - but that's as may be.

Saturday 3rd July 4.40 pm

Very hot today. Quite the hottest we have had for a long time. The flies worry the horses. There seem to be tons and tons of them. Luckily the horses get shade during the day.

All the men have been to some baths a couple of miles away and I trust enjoyed it. Most of them certainly look a lot cleaner.

Jones and I are messing with 'B' Company here and they do mess some!

Champagne most nights, plenty of variety of food. All food from home is pooled in a Company Mess.

Hallo - here comes one of my wagons back from Ordnance - wonder if he's got any tackle for me. As a matter of fact I get supplied very well with things for the horses. Nosebags are a big item and they get so torn and knocked about. The horses paw them etc. when on. One horse did in four in four feeds.

There have been some big bods around here today. Our Divisional General came and had a look at the lines, and also some of the top dogs have been playing around. Fortunately I did not happen to bump into any of 'em.

Sunday 4th July 10.40 pm

We have moved twenty miles and we shall be in the trenches again soon and wonderfully good ones also, I am told.

Wednesday 7th July 11 am

I have not the least idea when we are to move. I thought

it might have been today but now there is a chance of us staying here another week. The Colonel and Major Knox have been around my lines but they had nothing to grouse about and in fact seemed very pleased.

Friday 9th July 11 am

I am sitting in state at Brigade HQ in sole charge. The clerks bring in messages etc. to be signed, otherwise I've nothing to do. There is a Divisional show on and Captain Lea is away and the Transport not wanted, so being available I have to be here until the gilded staff return. There is nothing to do so I am having a slack morning. I think I'll give myself a couple of weeks' leave!

I am going into the nearest town, leaving here at six, just for a joy ride.

Leslie and his company are up on the hill, some way above us, in a fairly big village.

Saturday 10th July 2.30 pm

There is plenty of 'fizz' here - not the quality one gets at home or the price and its too sweet.

Wednesday 14th July 9.15 am

We came about eight miles the night before last. All the Battalion save one company are out on the field next to this and have made shelters with their ground sheets. Looks topping - quite a small city. I have a wagon sail to sleep under and five of A company's officers - there is just room for six of us.

*'The chaps would not believe at first that I'd been
fool enough to take Dodd on'*

I had some fun last night. The men in the next field,
our company fellows, got the 'gloves' to work, so I went
and had a look. I was always very fond of the 'gloves',
although of very little use with them. After several pairs
had been at it, all rather half hearted or fooling, I got
fed up so took my coat off and asked who'd come in. A
call went up for Dodd. He won the middle weight at
Witham and is about my height but bigger and broader.
Anyway - in for a penny in for a pound - we shook hands
and began.

Of course he could do almost what he liked with me,
but we had a good round and hit quite hard. He did not
get off free by any means. I put in one or two now and
again that he did not expect. We had a two-minute
round, one-minute rest and then another two-minute
round. The final time we went at it a little harder and
had a few bouts of quite good boxing.

My guard is too weak though. Luckily I can stand
being hit. Just before the final minute my nose began to

bleed. When I got back to the Mess the chaps would not believe at first that I'd been fool enough to take Dodd on.

I couldn't say 'no' though could I with two Companies standing around?!

Wednesday 14th July 3.30 pm

I had to send some 15 miles to get the post today making 30 miles in all. I am seated on the ground under the wagon sheet. Cyril has started out again. They will be glad to have him back in the 8th. His captain is in charge of the bomb company and would like to have Cyril to look after the 8th Battalion Platoon.

The bally rain has begun to come in on my bed so I must cover it up.

Thursday 15th July

Well - I had the 'gloves' on again tonight. I did not mean to but could not resist. Same man to fight. We had two good rounds. I've got a black eye, or expect to have in the morning. I gave him a fair amount of bumps and skinned his nose. He came in a little strong towards the end of the second round - tried to rush me but I gave him five lefts in succession - one each time he rushed so stayed his blows some.

It created much enjoyment to the onlookers and me. I find I am really much better with the gloves than I thought - I am the only officer to have them on up to now. I hope it will give some of the others a lead. They are fond of telling everyone how much they know etc.

Haven't heard if Cyril has arrived. I do not believe he has. We shall be fairly near the 8th tomorrow night, so I shall hear soon.

At 12 o'clock last night it came down in torrents. Luckily I had advised 'A' Company to sleep in the mess and let my fellows have the use of the sheet we had. They groused some but were mighty glad after.

The Company chaps are running races etc. and quite enjoying life.

Sunday 18th July, 10 am

As we are moving again mid-day there is no post out. Church Parade is on but there is plenty for my men to do without church parades.

I had a topping bath yesterday - quite the best since we came out. There is a mine here - well several all around - and they have shower baths for the miners and baths for the seniors, so the men all had shower baths and didn't we all enjoy them! Most of the officers had baths - great big ones and plenty of water.

Monday 19th July 8 pm

We arrived here this morning, having moved eighty or ninety miles by train and marching from 1.20 pm yesterday to 5 am.

We are all sleeping out - no one is in billets. Topping weather at present but cold nights and heavy dew.

The cake from home came in very useful today as one can get little or nothing in the food line here or anything else for that matter.

An R.E. Sub had tea with us, followed by all his R.E. Company officers - six all told. They had just arrived on this field and were jolly glad to find cake ready for them.

The A.S.C. are also here and have a gramophone going most of the time.

We are quite a compact little camp. The Battalion are in an orchard by the village.

Ah - Jones is making an omelette with some eggs I managed to get. Having put that away safely I shall get to bed.

We may be here for some time.

Wednesday 21st July 8.55 am

We move behind the trenches today. Cyril has not arrived as yet. He may be somewhere at the Base Depot.

Thursday 22nd July 12.15 pm

I asked Major Knox where I was on the list for leave for yesterday. I'm not last at least - as those who have been away sick etc. come last, having had some rest. Captain Sutton should have gone a week ago.

At present we are all under trees and around me are seven or eight officers al writing as they sit on the ground and lean against valises.

I have to send the horses three miles to water - six miles there and back - so I am only watering twice a day instead of three.

The 1/5th are getting into billets here at the moment. I think we will move on to the next village and the transport may be further back. It will be quite strange to settle down again. We certainly seem to have been wandering about long enough. We have covered a few miles in the last few weeks.

I have a servant now, apart from my groom. I spoke to the Colonel and he arranged it for me.

We are the first English in this part of the line. The folk hereabout have never seen English troops before. They seem rather frightened of us, although I have had nothing to do with any here up to now.

We got in at 10.20 last night and I was in bed by 12 when it started to rain. I do not know how long the rain went on as I went off to sleep pretty quickly. I put my valise cover well over my head and the oil sheet over the whole, so no water came in.

Friday 22nd July, 2.20 pm

Cyril is still at Le Havre and he is not likely to move up yet.

The flies here are just awful, millions everywhere you go. One can't have a meal without swarms settling over everything.

I was with Captain Lea all morning. We went to see a new place for Transport to save the three mile trudge for watering. I expect to move tomorrow.

Jones is up with the Battalion. I am seated outside in quite a nice wee garden and feeling miles from the show. They are rotten villages here - all fly eaten and dirty.

Leave is NOT on again yet but I should say it will be soon.

A quaint old woman has just been jabbering here.

She's left in charge and is moving all round. When I asked for the key to open the garden door she said she hadn't got one. I found I could easily force the door without damaging it and now she's found it open she has produced the key. She is quite friendly now. I can hear her laughing. My man is speaking English and she replies in French and neither know a word of what the other is saying.

We are well in the wilds here, with no big towns nearby, just tiny villages made up of farms.

It has been some time since I was able to write in comfort at a table with a chair.

The gnats are a pest here and the bites a nuisance as one keeps taking the top off when shaving. The bites come up during the night. It's all part of the fun - 'dodging gnat bites when shaving' is a good game.

Sunday 25th July

I like being on my own for a while. Jones is at his stores with the Company and is staying there.

I have a note from Cyril. He says he is in charge of a Company 280 strong and four subalterns. He longs to No. 1 Trench Digging Battalion.

My Battalion go into the trenches tonight, first time in these new ones, so shall be late in. It will be quite like old times to go up to the trench dumps once again.

10.30 pm

Just back and we got our transport into position and clear in fine style. The 1/5th I met going up as I came away, some time behind my last pair of horses.

Tomorrow I've to arrange for all the Brigade Transports to move down to the river on to the ground which Lea and I looked at a few days ago. I will take the other Transport officers tomorrow morning at 8.30 to see just where they are to go.

Thursday 29th July, 10.15 am

We moved back yesterday a mile or so and someone else took our old patch. It is very hot today a real scorcher. It's time we had some decent weather and got rid of this rain.

We have quite a nice patch here - the flies are awful as I said before. Everywhere - in thousands. One of the men came back yesterday and says he noticed the difference as soon as he landed. There are some flies in England but none compared to this.

We are two or three hours' run from Paris and five or six from town, although as things are it takes the best part of a day to get across. When Leave does arrive one should get five clear days in England - hopefully 4½ at home.

Friday 30th July 11 am

I haven't much to do this morning. We fetch the Battalion out tonight. They have been in well over time. I believe Transport will stay here now for a while. The 1/5th are to come into the next field - or rather 'orchard'.

I went into the trenches yesterday as one can go in by day. You have 15 minutes' walk from the entrance of the communication trench to the first Company. HQ are up there too - and about 25 minutes brings you into the firing line. I did not get that far. There has been some work put in up there. The Bosh did most of it. It was fine yesterday so the trenches were hard and dry, but a spot of rain and they are soon ankle deep in mud.

Its difficult for me to give you an idea of just what they are like. It's a huge network of deep trenches, wide enough to pass anyone and at least 10 ft. deep.

The Battalion had only one man slightly damaged up to last night, the 1/5th had three killed and eleven wounded when a shell dropped on them.

Saturday 31st July 2 pm

Leave is for the men only. The Divisional General says we are too short of officers for any to go on leave - only one per Battalion can go at any time.

I have not done much today save routine work. I was up at 7 am having slept like a top. We got back from the trenches about 11 pm. Following breakfast today I had a look at the horses and got the wagons away to draw supplies etc. and then went with one to get some green forage for the gees. A plot was allotted for us and we have to cut and collect it, so I amused myself helping to cut and became jolly hot as the sun was well up.

I have been doing odd jobs, looking at the horses and the cook house up to lunch time. Then I spent time censoring letters and went to the lines to get my gee and one for Captain Peyton. The vet arrived as I left and I arranged for 'skinny Lizzie' to go. She's worn out.

The vet kept me talking for ten minutes and then we

went to the Battalion about a mile away. I met the Colonel, who tells me one of his horses has to go. It grieves me.

I was at the Battalion up to 4.45 pm and Captain Sutton came back with me for tea. Just as we dismounted Bushill and Murray arrived and we were able to have quite a merry little tea party. They went back on a passing wagon.

Bank Holiday Monday 2nd August

Early yesterday morning about 3.15 am I was routed out and had to take the transport to the Battalion 'at once' but it was an alarm which came to naught.

The Battalion are two miles away. We settled down there and then had orders to remain for the night or longer. The Battalion are all sleeping out so I looked round to see where I could sleep. I found 'D' Company Bushill and Copper hadn't a place. The rest had a wagon sheet Jones had put up the night before. Eventually I fetched another off a wagon so we had a good place all right. We came back here today. I've a topping billet this time.

7th Battalion Royal Warwickshire Regiment.

The under mentioned Lieutenants to be temporary Captains:

H. R. Hoskins
C. Murray

The under mentioned Second Lieutenants to
be temporary Lieutenants:

LP. H. W. Hicks,
H. P. Sherwood.

Thursday 5th August

I had not heard that Officers was on. None of our
Battalion are going yet, save NCOs and men.

A bally General may be coming around my lines a
little later, so I had better be getting along there.

Friday 6th August 2 am

I have just got to bed. We've had one of those delightful
false alarms 'Stand to' at 9.25 pm. Then we all went to
see the General and say 'how do' and back we came
again. All my fellows had to pull their huts down and
now it's raining hard, just to finish off any who are still
in good temper.

As usual there was a decent mix-up, everyone
wondering what to do, very few doing anything right and
the General very pleased at having disturbed the whole
Brigade. Just as everyone was in a good mess he says 'now
sort yourselves and go back to bed'. it's a great game.

Being Battalion Transport Officer I have to report to
HQ and the TO sergeants report to me. One didn't
report at all. One man did with his transport present.
My Sergeant couldn't report as it would leave nobody
to see to the wagons. Then I heard the Brigadier say that

all could go back to bed if the transport were all up. Next he called for me to know if all was correct. I forgot the sergeant who hadn't come and I reported 'Yes'. Good thing it was dark!

He seemed pleased and away we've all come and its raining hard.

It's a great game, everyone gets so excited - Majors, Adjutants and Colonels all foam at the mouth and shout. Really and truly if one looks on the humorous side there's lots of fun.

I have been up to see Captain Lea. The General I understand was delighted with everything, so that's all right.

Cruggins whom I saw at the Brigade today tells me I was in the paper yesterday so perchance you have seen it. Up to now the Orderly room has not said anything. In any case I shall go back to a Company as I see the Brigadier has issued orders that no Captain shall be either Transport, Signalling, or Machine Gun Officers. All Captains therefore join a Company.

I shall hate it. Still we are at War - we aren't here for fun.

Copper Murray is also a Captain over the head of one fellow. I have called all the Transport Officers together for 4 pm today so as to tell them about last night and make it all clear just what they should have done.

One thing is I shall not have so much to do on Alarms with a Company.

I shall hate leaving the Transport which I've had since September - nearly a full year.

Leave begins for officers once more I see.

Saturday 8th August 4.20 pm

We move to an old position today as the Battalion are moving in, so it throws things out a bit. I am no longer Battalion Transport Officer. Morgan is to take over that role. Still the Battalion has said nothing about my going on this journey. Saw John Leslie yesterday. He and Bryan rode over to congratulate me. I went over and had supper with them.

Sunday 9th August 10.30 am

Up to now all has been about life BEHIND the trenches. Tomorrow will be life IN the Trenches.

I saw fellows up to their knees in mud. Some poor chaps were quite exhausted after eight days there. The mud is awful. I will go in tonight when we take up the rations. I shall ride up on Dick. For the time being no one is taking on the Transport. Jones is to run it, so old Dick will be spare for a while.

I am to go to 'D' company to begin with. I am delighted at that as it is my pals Bushill and Copper.

It's a rotten day - very dull and close with rain threatening. I do not know if 'D' Company is in the firing line or not. In any case we are still some way from the Bosh. I shall be glad now when I've got up there and settled in. I don't like all this hanging around.

Life in the trenches

2.35 pm
IN THE TRENCHES

I'm afraid I shall get bored some on this game although there is plenty to do. I am with 'C' Company Captain Mason for the present. The Orderly Room changed its mind about 'D'.

I am not sure I shall stay here though but since all the other Companies have two Captains now I almost expect I shall have to. Major Knox has been in and asked me if being 'out' so long made me nervous of the shells and bullets. I told him that up to date I'd not noticed them much.

I am glad to say the trenches have dried up some when I came in but a few days ago they were 1½ ft deep in water and mud. Some men can be seen in a pair of boots and a jacket, others minus the boots! I can see several things need to be done to improve this dugout, which is already very comfy.

I have not had a wash or shave yet today. Murray and I are having a competition to see which of us can grow the most fluff while in. He had a good day's start on me as I had a good shave yesterday.

As we are in the firing line we are not allowed to undress so I just lay down as I came in with my feet in a sack to keep the mud together. I turned in at 11 pm and slept until 6 am. I should have been out 3 am for the Stand-to but Mason did not wake me as I had a rotten head last night.

Luckily I got Mason to have the entrance to our dugout cleared and places dug to take the water. They were finished just as the rain came and are now ¼ full.

One fellow was buried today - all save his head. He was cutting out a hole to sleep in when the top gave way. He's not much hurt. 'Water, water, everywhere and not a drop to drink'.

I shall quite enjoy 'draining' - reminds me of sandcastles on the beach.

9 pm

It has been raining cats and dogs and lightning and thunder - a very gay evening. As I write the water is coming through the roof like fun and we look like being drowned out before morning. I am off to see if we've anything big to catch some of the rain in.

Last night was a brute. Today there is mud and slush everywhere. Parts of the trench fell in and - to improve matters - half the men's dugouts also fell in. Luckily no one was buried.

When I went around this morning I saw two men digging out their belongings. Transport work seems far away now.

The sick have just arrived. The doctor has to wade around to all companies per day. The working party arrived, carrying their trousers and socks, as they had to wade through the mud which comes above the knees.

I am glad to say here at present it is only just above our boots.

The sun is out and its quite hot, so at least various garments can be dried.

Wednesday 11th August 12 noon

Things are quiet here. A few shells pass over both ways and there is the occasional rifle fire.

Apparently I may have to go to 'A' Company eventually and Captain Sutton will come here to command. I am told we are going to get four new officers shortly.

Friday 13th August 3 pm

I am not able to find out when I am due leave. The list is kept low and quiet for some unknown reason.

I went to bed last night at 12.15 or thereabouts and rose at 6 am. I say 'to bed' - that is I lie down on the straw complete with boots and all togs on with my greatcoat thrown over me. I must say it is extraordinary how well one can sleep like that though.

Saturday 14th August

Several things occurred last night. Two of our trained chaps who throw the bombs came to borrow our revolvers. When they returned they had not seen or done anything in particular. Then later while some of our men were out messing about with the barbed wire protection in front three of them were hit - and all with the same bullet. One of our Listening Posts spied a Bosh close in amongst our wire and shot him. Two of our stretchers were occupied so the 1/8th fetched the German's body and his tunic and papers were taken to our Battalion HQ. The 8th had the pleasure of burying the body. So in a way the war was in our favour last night.

We are busy making the trenches more tenable and stronger for fighting in the event we are attacked. No doubt the enemy are doing the same across the way!

Sunday 15th August.

The damned Bosh have put nearly 100 shells at and over us today. We've replied with much the same number.

We will be occupied tomorrow in getting things clean and all the mud scraped off. Then we will be on working parties each day for a while. I bet I shall get fed up with all this. I shall revel in a good bath.

Monday 16th August 2.30 pm

I've been seeing about equipment this morning. I wish

those in command would make up their minds as to where I am to be. My view is that the trenches are not too bad a place to be in and although I was not used to the shelling I did not find it too dreadful. If only I had a gee when out I'd be A1.

Tuesday 17th August 9.15 am

I have a meeting in the next village soon about some billeting so I shall get a ride - on Dick with luck. We are out of the trenches for eight days at a time. Yesterday was spent cleaning up. There's a parade at 7.30 am and then a working party will be away digging a few miles off. The men won't be back before 6 pm. This is to be the routine each day we are out I believe. I was to go with one party but the meeting I have to attend upset it, thank goodness.

Thursday 19th August 10.20 am

Here I am in the middle of a big wood with a working party but where they are I am not sure. They are somewhere making hurdles. I am sitting writing to pass the time. We will be here until 12.30 and again from 2 to 4 pm. I was here yesterday also and got drenched to the skin - luckily it is only ten minutes walk from our billets. The working party have cut about 1,000 trees or more down.

We had a concert last evening. The RAMC came over and gave quite a good show.

Hopefully I will see Leslie this afternoon. I have not

done so since he came back. I have to go near to where he is to pay some men.

Friday 20th August 2.45 pm

I sat up last night until about midnight playing cards. There was quite a furious cannonade to our left last evening and we thought we might get hauled out.

News has just arrived that the Colonel is not satisfied with sanitation in and about the billets so I have to go and 'smell around', rouse someone and make some show in case the Colonel does the round again. I wish he'd had a better lunch and slept better.

Duck for supper last night and it was simply topping - done to a turn and it only cost 4.5 frs.

Sunday 22nd August 12.45 pm

Breakfast was late and then I went and nosed around all the billets and found them quite respectable and clean. Poor news today. Leave is stopped again, so don't look for me now until the beginning of October - or even later now.

Tuesday 23rd August 2.50 pm

One of the men is having his teeth attended to so I am in charge for the time being. Ah - Leave I am told is ON again.

'C' company is in reserve and well back. We form working parties, two during the day and one at night.

We hadn't been out for half an hour before an officer and one platoon were asked to work up to 2 am. I went but I knocked off at 1 am. We were all pretty well fagged out after the march to get to our destination. The job is to get wood out of old German dugouts - those trenches must have been hell on earth for there is not a complete dugout to be found anywhere. The trenches are all smashed in. There are big holes and complete havoc.

There is a rumour we may be moving to a fresh line again and some of Kitchener's troops will come in here.

I have spent the morning improving my dugout and I have made it much better with the help of a table. I had shrapnel burst over me yesterday but no damage done. Our folk are just beginning today to put a few 'iron rations' over for the benefit of the Bosh.

Wednesday 24th August 12.40 pm

We may be moving again. I shall be sorry to leave these particular trenches as they are not too bad now we've put some work into them and got trench gratings down.

It's been lovely weather all this week.

I had a good bath today in a knocked-down village - with warm water too.

Friday 27th August 12.5 pm

A real summer day as hot as can be. Thank goodness we've nothing to do. I shall sleep under the shade of the old apple tree after dinner.

We are in the reserve trenches and it does not make

much difference to the amount of work. As a matter of fact I'm having the slackest time since I arrived in France. I am wondering what the next place will be like for I understand them to be topping trenches.

Our Colonel has gone away sick so Major Knox looks like being unable to go on leave as he'll be in charge.

'I shall sleep under the shade of the old apple tree after dinner.

Sunday 29th August

None of us officers have had any letters today.

We are not to go into the trenches again for some days

yet. I've been over some French trenches today. They are real top hole places and supposed to be about the best on the line.

During supper a wee girl aged about three and a bit years came in and sat down at our table, quite at her ease. She started by having a good look around and selected a box of matches which we had to take from her. We gave her a 'bull's eye' sweetie instead. Fowler opened a box of Gold Flake and gave her the picture, which - by the way - she did not value at all. Her little brother aged about seven was with her too and Fowler gave him a fag. If you please the child wanted one also. Then he lit them both, but we would not let him smoke in here so they went into a room where Ma and the others were. Now you would not believe this but that little mite of three smoked the cigarette to the very end just like a grown-up. We did laugh - she kept us amused the whole of supper.

I had a topping ride on old Dick today. I really enjoyed it and I think Dick did too.

Monday 30th August 9.10 am

I had breakfast and then inspected the billets. Two of the men are on the working party so I am not very busy this morning. I hope I may get over to see Leslie today. I am sending a messenger along to find out when he'll be in so I should get at him this time unless he's just too far distant.

I visited another village nearby yesterday. The church has been knocked to pieces, the spire has gone and the roof and part of the walls knocked in - a sad sight. The only part not touched is a large cross with the figure of our Lord. There have been shells all around it and not one has touched it. It stands twelve or fourteen feet high.

It is the prettiest village I have been to but, as usual, it is all smashed up.

'The church had been knocked to pieces, the spire gone and the roof and walls knocked in - a sad sight'.

Tuesday 31st August 1.35 pm

When we are out with the working parties we like to imagine, for practice, the enemy - it's a much safer way to attack. We are usually working back from the trenches, so that anyone who becomes over excited may not overrun the mark and charge the real enemy, thereby upsetting the peaceful run of things at present. Just think how upset they would be if Private Jones suddenly jumped into the middle of their lunch. I mean to say he might hurt someone and it might not be easy to convince them he was not really attacking them and he was just out for practice and had overrun the mark. He would explain that he must be back in time for tea and he is also due for a bomb throwing course.

We imagine there is a great amount of barbed wire to get hung up on, thereby causing a tailor much hard labour.

It's a much more gentlemanly attack without the wire.

I feel wonderfully well today!

Wednesday 1st September 1 pm

There was a battle last night and it went very nicely and we won. We took quite a bit of ground but nearly lost the Colonel and the Major through a cow getting excited at our approaching victory. The cow broke loose and made for the Colonel and Major. Half a dozen brave and noble lads made a circle with the firm intention of holding out to the last. The cow made off to the nearest pile of fresh cut and stacked wheat (and oh - the joy with which she demolished that stack, tossing trusses in all directions). Of course she was really making sure there were no Bosh underneath!

In the minds of some of the men this harmless cow became a great fierce bull and I have heard many versions of the incident related.

I am going to have a look again at the new trenches this afternoon - those that we are to be taking over from the French. I am not sure when we are due in.

The general advance seems to have gone much faster here.

*'The cow made off to the nearest pile of fresh
cut and stacked wheat'*

I've just been awakened to go on patrol and it is a job to keep my eyes open. I had a fairly close shave yesterday. Fowler and I were on our way to the kitchens when they began to shell a house, just about 50 yards to our left. We were in a fairly deep communication trench. One or two shell came 'swish' and 'bang' - then one came really close - just a few yards away. We ducked low and got smothered with earth. Fowler was not low enough and the explosion knocked him down. The shells do kick up a noise when they are low like that.

I had a good day for my birthday. We met the Colonel at 10 am and went for a staff ride - just officers mounted - to carry out an attack.

In the afternoon I had a good look around here with Dumas and a Sergeant or two, arriving back at 6 pm when I was due to pay the Company. My two subalterns told me they were going out to supper so I sent down to 'B' company to ask Ash to invite me there and I sent down two ducks and some vegetables which had arrived that day from home. I told Ash to get in some champagne as it was my birthday.

We had a very merry party - all us 'Assassins' - nine or ten of us. The party did not break up until after midnight.

Real topping A1 dugouts and trenches these, all boarded. There is a stove, table, three chairs and an armchair, an iron bedstead and a window curtain - all complete. I shall be sorry to give it up to Mason when he returns from leave. The dugouts for the men are good as well. Each dugout holds ten or twelve easily and there is plenty of room to lie down.

Wednesday 8th September 6.35 pm

Mason returned last night. As I sit here in my dugout, not the trenches, I am feeling very comfy. The stove is alight and two candles and everything laid out in a most orderly fashion.

Friday 10th September 12.30 pm

On Monday next I start for home! If all goes well I shall be with you Tuesday morning for breakfast. I had the orders not half an hour or so ago

Leslie came in just after. He is looking well.

We are due in the trenches today but as Mason is back I'll have an easier time of it.

Telegram - Folkestone Pier -
Monday 13th September 12.28 pm

Just in - expect me some time this evening at The Grange .

Wednesday 22nd September 6.45 pm

Well I am back safe and sound. We are out of the trenches at present. I haven't the least interest in anything here yet. I do not know what we are to do here in this place. We've not been just here before for rest and recuperation.

Saturday 25th September 5.20 pm

A slack time. I haven't caught up with Leslie yet. I sent him a family note as soon as I arrived as one of their officers was in the same train and going straight up to the Battalion.

We go in tomorrow and it has rained most of the time since I returned.

We are in Reserve this time so I shall not have so much work to do.

Tuesday 28th September 12.30 pm

I have spent the morning cleaning up the trenches, getting out the water from the 'sump' holes. The 8th Company who were in here before us left them all full up so that the trenches were getting into a rotten state but things are improving now. I finished cleaning at about 4.30 pm. The trenches have not had so much attention for some weeks. You would not believe the amount of water we have cleared.

Some good news this morning. I wonder what news there is from the Dardanelles. Has it been in the papers about the Transport full of troops being sunk? I heard of this while coming out.

It is a poor day cold and damp. I shall get a fire going towards evening to air my sleeping area.

Wednesday 29th September 9 pm

I am seated here in my dugout while the others play cards next door. I have been here all evening with a wood fire and it is very comfortable.

We have had an officer and 25 men come up from the Reserves. I do not believe Cyril has come as I have not heard so.

Following all my hard work yesterday the place was full of water again this morning as it rained heavily last evening so we had to set about clearing it all up again.

Friday October 1st 12.40 pm

There is to be a route march today. Luckily our Company is on a working party so we miss it.

I've been out on 'Dick' this morning to look at the wire defences. The horse was fine and fresh and we had quite a good hour or so. I also had a good look around the horses' lines this morning as well. Most of the animals are looking well. It needs someone to take them over all the same as a Sergeant cannot get things done like an officer can. Payton is worked to death. I tell him he's a fool to do it all as it's more than a one-man job.

We had a bomb drop near us yesterday about 50 yds away from where I was - no one was hurt and only a small piece of wall was knocked down.

Oh - there go the other three companies for their Route March, God bless 'em.

Sunday 3rd October, 8.10 pm

Had a good ride on Dick today of about sixteen miles. We only missed being in the thick of it though by about five minutes, so that was a near one!

Tuesday 5th October, 5.45 pm

There is to be an impromptu concert tonight for our Company. I have arranged it all and just seen the Colonel. It starts at 6 pm. I do wish I could sing as I would have loved to have helped. I have had a drum sent out which arrived today and is creating some fun. We have several men who can play. Our band will consist of a drum, a harmonium, three mouth organs, a whistle and a flute. It looks like being a merry evening.

This sort of event really cheers the men up. It's been raining all day and they were all wet through this morning. One has to do what one can to keep them amused and cheerful.

'Our band will consist of a drum, harmonium, three mouth organs, a whistle and a flute'

Wednesday 6th October, 3.40 pm

Glad to report the concert was a great success. It really went off A1 and everyone enjoyed it and had a merry old time. I still went round all the billets (sheds) and saw they all got to bed and settled down without trouble - and then I went around again just to make sure. I'd have hated for any of them to have got into trouble.

It was odd though coming out of that happy room as the first thing one was conscious of was the boom of the guns up north.

The Colonel and Major Knox came in to see us and say a few words. We all sang 'For he's a jolly good fellow' of course, accompanied by our 'band'. Funny really - only a few hours before they had all been cussing the Colonel up the hill and down dale for making them do a practice attack with full packs. Such is life! Anyway we had a jolly two hours and I think the merriest as a Company since Witham.

I have spent three days on a bomb course and finished today. Every officer and man in our Battalion has to go on a bomb course and very wise too, so then we'll all be able to handle them if necessary.

Don't take any notice of the yarns published in the *Leamington Courier* of 1st October as it is all rot. It appears to have come from our Battalion too. Some ass trying to swank. It must have gone through in a green envelope which we do not see, they are supposed to be for family affairs only.

Thursday 7th October 2.45 pm

We undertook a wonderful attack this morning and took a number of trenches in 20 minutes!

Saturday 9th October 2.15 pm

While writing up the diary last night they began to drop a few big shells which fairly shook the dugout. I thought they were dropping close but actually they were 500 or so yards away in 'B' Company. Only one did any damage.

I have a stove going here and we are getting quite hot. It's a small dugout with two of us in it and the window and door shut. It has quite a useful number of cracks though, which permits some air to enter.

Brian Ash has been recommended for good service in the field - why and for what no one knows at present.

Sunday 10th October 4 pm

Leave is to begin again, so those who have not been should be feeling pleased. We had orders for us to move to the fighting area cancelled five minutes before the time to move.

We have had a mess dug out here, a good roomy place with plenty of light.

We have been 'strafing' the Bosh this afternoon. We spotted a machine gun and had the guns firing on it so I hope it has upset a gun or two.

I have written to Pop to send me out a couple of

lamps for use in our dugouts - one for the mess and one for my dugout. We can get paraffin and candles, which cost us anything up to 7 francs a week now.

Tuesday 12th October 1.10 pm

We have no less than five officers attached to us at present and have to feed the bally lot. It comes expensive and stores run out in no time. We can't get them to mess themselves as we have them up for instruction and a good deal is learned while talking at meal times. They are a decent lot - they are an Irish group and should make a fine lot of soldiers.

Wednesday 13th October 6.15 pm

We have had some fun today I can tell you. You should see us now - Fowler and myself away down in a cellar where we are making our abode. Owing to the new arrangements we have had to come out of our dugout in the front line and have not had time to get things straight yet.

We had a good old strafe with the Bosh yesterday- only nine well behind the line slightly hurt.

Thursday 14th October 3.30 pm

Our cellar is coming into shape now. I have had a stove put in and I am trying to keep the heat in and the smoke outside. Last night we were properly smoked out with an open fire but we were comfy as some of the men found a couple of iron beds - one is a double bed so with our valises we did A1.

I want to get the walls cleaned and then whitened. We will have to borrow a few chairs from somewhere. We have a table and I intend to put up another fixed one. It will not be such a bad billet then.

An Irishman in the trench the other day was on sentry duty with our fellows at night and asked one man if he would like to have a shot with his rifle. Our man said 'Yes' and took it and found it was not loaded. He told the Irishman 'but the bally thing's not loaded.!' The Irishman replied 'Ah - to be sure - I thought there was something wrong.'

'Ah - to be sure -
I thought there was
something wrong'

Saturday 18th October 4.30 pm

Right well we are out again and ready for a rest. I believe Leslie is to be just across the road from us so I hope to see quite a good amount of him this time out.

A big shell has burst somewhere near - one of those big chaps. Several have put in today and two of them close to where we were yesterday, one not twenty yards away.

I have seen Leslie two or three times today - also Jack Cooper - and I am feeding tonight with John at his Company HQ.

Tuesday 19th October, 4.30 pm

I went over to Leslie for supper and a topping good one it was too. We enjoyed a game of poker and had a jolly evening.

The weather has turned chilly the last few days and one is quite glad to have a fire going when indoors. We are sure to get some real cold weather soon. We are to be provided with whale oil and everyone will have to oil their feet and legs before going into the trenches. The cold is worst on the men who have to stand on sentry duty for several hours at a time, in all weathers.

I have hopes of seeing you all before Christmas and sitting down to Christmas dinner with peace declared. Is that too much to ask? I will not give up hope yet - unlikely as the prospect of peace seems.

Saturday 23rd October, 5.40 pm

Another new billet for when we are out. It should be A1 when finished but all the doors and windows had gone before we took over and some of the ones we have put in do not fit exactly! Also window frames but without glass don't seem to keep the cold out - even with wire netting on! I have managed to get some canvas to cover the windows and our Company bricklayer has just put in a fireplace, which is excellent, and also one for the kitchen.

Sunday 24th October

Glory! You should have had a look at me at 6 am I was on duty from 5 - 9 last night and from this morning - then I go on again. We are an officer short so get an extra hour.

From 8 pm till this morning it just rained like mad. I had my fleece lined Burberry and Macintosh over it, but my puttees were soaked and let the water into my boots. My Mac is a right sight, as rubbing against the sides of the trench has coloured it a pretty brown.

The trenches are in a wonderful mess. Here I am in the cellar with lamp alight and a brazier with wood burning in it - half the smoke still stays in the cellar and the rest condescends to clear out., As I sit here I am just below the level as the smoke all goes to the top. It makes my eyes run a bit but it's better than sitting shivering.

Thursday 28th October 4.55 pm

Rain, rain, rain, rain.

Sunday 31st October 3.15 pm

I have been out with the wiring parties the last two nights putting up wire in front of our lines. I went out with the covering party and with another man went 30 yards beyond, so we were a hundred yards or so ahead of the lines. At one point I was sure I saw someone moving towards us through the grass. Maybe they were there, or maybe not - it could have been thick clumps of grass. We stayed there about 10 or 15 minutes and

'A gramophone has come for the men so we had it in and a pal and I danced to 'Dreaming''

It's the furthest I have been out yet and the third time. A jolly good way to pass the time - patrol goes quickly then. I've now been nearly all over the front of our section. I just want to do the left tonight.

A gramophone has come for the men so we had it in and a pal and I danced to 'Dreaming'. Some show!

Monday November 1st 12.20 am

I have just returned from patrol and am now ready for bed. I saw the wiring party at another place - everything tonight is very quiet.

It is raining hard and has done so for the last 24 hours or more. Everything is wonderfully wet and to make things really nice we've no fire.

I will go to 'B' company for a game of cards this evening. I have not played for some time.

Friday 5th November 3.15 pm

We have been on a route march since 12.30. Fancy this being November 5th and there is nothing doing. Our guns have done a little 'strafing' for luck.

The men are all keeping very fit - I really can't see how they manage to keep so well.

I had a topping ride yesterday on Dick. It does me good to get a blow now and again. Both Dick and I enjoyed the outing.

Saturday 6th November 4.25 pm

Cyril writes to say he is to come back to the 1/8th shortly and he seems pleased, so I hope to be seeing something of him.

We have a new fireplace built today and now have a topping fire and this room feels quite warm for once.

I have sent for the band to come and give us a few selections. They really are first class and I am sending home to Pop's for a few more mouth organs. Mason, Fowler and Dumas are all trying to practise at the same time and only one of them can play at all - so there is lots of noise!

Sunday 7th November 6.30 pm

When Fowler and I danced the other night it was in an old damaged house where we feed when our Company is in the trenches. Our cellar is below. It is a rotten cold room upstairs on the ground floor with no glass in the windows and we usually eat in a topcoat.

One of our men has been awarded a French medal - and also Captain Lea. I am glad Lea has been awarded something.

This afternoon we have had some sports for the men. It was just our company and the games created great amusement between them.

Tuesday 9th November 5.20 pm

Here we are - in again, all alive and kicking. Cyril arrived and came in just after we arrived here. He looks very fit and says he's glad to be back and it's a bit like getting home. He's missed his leave. I was told also that he was sorry to say he believed Cyril has just missed being made a Captain.

Uthwaite has arrived today so I imagine he will take over Transport which will help matters. Another new officer has also arrived for 'A' and 'B', I am told. We could do with another.

Wednesday 10th November 2.50 pm

We are having a great time. It rained all last night and has been on and off all today. The trenches are a right picture, some of the best examples in mud and water you would wish to see. One day's rain means a week's work to clean up as the sides of the trenches play a nice little game slipping further down, just as one is getting things shipshape.

Our one consolation is that from what we can see the opposition are worse off than us as they are lower down.

Our chaps are well fitted out and everything is being done to keep them well. Last night I came off patrol at 2 am having been on duty since 10 pm and I turned in in the trench. Fowler is also here as he's living up here. He had the lower berth so I took the top and was not all pleased as it is so narrow. The rain began to drip through - missed my narrow bed and caught Fowlers on both sides so he got fairly damp. He's put an oil sheet up now and has already gathered about a bucket full.

I have a new dugout and it is a topping place and dry up to date, as it is newer than some of the others. I shall take up my abode there now and be quite happy.

Our little dog caught a rat almost as big as himself last night. We have two or three cats up here also.

11.50 pm

I wish it was 2 am so I could go to sleep. I am now up in the front line and have quite a good fire going. There is a Private with me. I always have him with me on patrol and when I am out in front. He says he likes the job as he gets off sentry work and the working parties during the day. He takes care of the food for his platoon ie. Orderly man.

I have big waders on now. At present they look fine with a good thick layer of mud up to the knee. The men are issued with the same type but they are not such a good make. At least waders give us a chance of keeping dry.

Thursday 11th November, 4.10 pm

Luckily for us two big shells dropped just outside our trenches today, while on our left they had two plump in. No one hurt but the trench is a mess.

My dugout gets beautifully warm so when I am wet I pop in and change. Then by the time I am wet again the first change is ready. Mind you, as a rule it is only boots and socks.

One of the chaps has developed a bad back and is walking like an old man today and the shells broke the windows of his dugout so he is feeling quite down.

Friday 12th November, 8.15 pm

Last night was a brute, it rained hard all night and nearly everywhere flooded. There is a high wind blowing. I was glad to get to bed some time about 4.15 am and slept like a top until 9.30.

Tonight I am trying a new arrangement so that the men have less time on sentry duty as they get so cold and wet standing in one place all the time.

Also I am on all night. We each do a whole night in turn and have three off. Supper comes up at 11 am with the hot tea the men have each night, and then they get the rum in the morning at 'stand down'.

We have a special place for the men to get their socks dried, rub their feet with oil and put long boots on for sentry duty.

Take a field and dig a trench 3 ft. wide at the top, 2' 6" at the bottom and 8 ft. deep. Fill it up two feet with a thick mud so that your feet go right through and stick. Then - a little way along - make it sloppy and a little deeper - and then you have our trenches! As fast as you clear up it falls down or rains and fills up again. But we just have to keep on keeping on.

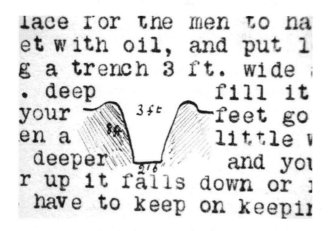

'Take a field and dig a trench… '

Monday 15th November, 4 pm

It's my night on tonight. We had a sharp frost last night so everything was white this morning and it seems there will be another frost tonight. At least it dries the trenches up so that we have been able to clear up a good amount today.

One of my men had a bullet through his cap today. It cut the head clean off the Antelope cap badge and came out at the top without touching his head. He was way back in the village too - it was just a stray shot.

Tuesday 16th November, 6.45 am

Snow! It started about 4.15 am and has not stopped, so now we can say we have been in all weathers. I should have been relieved at 6.30 by Mason.

3.45 pm

I was finally relieved at 8.30 a.m. some two hours late by Dumas, Mason having decided to remain in bed.

A circular note has just come from our Corps Commander saying he is fully aware of the hardships and discomforts and the hard work caused by the wet weather (and now the snow).

He says he '*I am glad to see that the situation has been met in the cheery manner characteristic of the true British soldier and congratulate the troops in the way in which they are overcoming their difficulties*'. He goes on to say that he hopes the troops ' *will not be so intent on making lives in the trenches comfortable that they will not be able to spare time to make the enemy's life uncomfortable, not to say completely unbearable'.*

You should have seen the men at stand-to this morning - snow falling and everything white with a mist hanging over the trenches opposite. Yet they were happy as sandboys singing away between occasional shots and shouting such things as 'Waiter, waiter, bring me a sausage'.

It's a funny thing how rain and snow seem to make the men sing! Our chief danger is frostbite in the feet. Unfortunately the drying place, like the rest of the dugouts, has let the rain in so last night I had the roof covered with iron sheets.

I guess this weather will confuse those who did not expect another winter show. While we are well looked after and prepared for it I do not believe they are over opposite.

Wednesday 17th November 5.45 am

This evening I have some topping mail. One postcard and five letters.

Leslie gets away on Sunday also Cyril and Bryan. I saw Cyril this morning bringing his platoon in. Also I saw Howkins who said 'By Jove, Bardie, you are looking wonderfully fit'.

I hear Tommy* is on the way out. Wouldn't it be great if the City Battalions came out to us for instruction.

Thursday 18th November, 3.40 pm

Out again and arrived in these dugouts last night. I am on a working party tonight up in our trenches. I had a clothes inspection this morning from 10 to 12. It is very important to keep the men's togs and boots repaired. Their hair also is much too long now in many cases, so I set two men on to cut and let them off parade for their trouble.

Friday 19th November, 5.30 pm

I have been with Uthwaite all afternoon at the Transport explaining various matters. Good news today - Payton tells me he is come to this company and he is senior to Mason. I believe he is to come next time we go in the trenches so I shall be moved and I may go to my old Company 'B', which would be fine.

Friday 26th November 2.30 pm

We had a lively 'strafe' last evening almost at mid-night. No one hurt but a few shells came bumping around. The Germans are sending a few over every now and then again today. A small one just fell behind my dugout.

Four of our men took a stroll over to the last night and brought some barbed wire back. We are closer here than I was in 'C' - about 200 or 150 yds here. Very useful fellows in this company - each ready to do his share and a bit more besides if required.

*FOOTNOTE Tommy was his younger brother, lost to the family many years ago.

More snow - quite thick for a bit - followed by rain.

The Lieutenants in this company are Gaussen, Hicks, Field and a new lad - Caley. I am quite the 'old man' of this lot.

Just outside here, not 800 yards from the Bosh, are ten of our lads playing football.

There is a very sharp frost last night which has not broken yet.

Oh dear - I have a pile of letters here to censor.

Sunday 28th November, 3.20 pm

We are getting some heavy shelling sent over to us today and last night. No one touched up to date. I have a small piece that fell at my feet just now when I was out.

Last night we had a wiring party out, as we often do. I was at the far end of the trench from where they were working when suddenly there was a burst of rapid machine gun fire - very savage - and I thought our party had been found, so off I popped to see. When I got outside I found them all correct and discovered the firing was further along the line. As the air is so clear and frosty it sounded closer than it was.

Monday 29th November, 2.25 pm

I think I am getting fatter - certainly the buttons on my coat are getting tight. I have a new servant - his name is Stone and he's looking after me very well.

Tuesday 30th November, 3.15pm

A few big shots are dropping just away from here, far enough away not to be too unpleasant.

Lawks! Last night was a beauty - rain and wind, dark as pitch. Fortunately I was not on duty until 1 am. The rain ceased at 1.30 am and the moon rose - so my luck was in again.

Wednesday 1st December 1915 3.45 pm

Not much happening, save this constant rain. Water everywhere, to be pumped away as best we can.

I have lit a fire and I am now being well smoked.

Cyril's company takes over each time now from us so when he's back I may get a look at him each time my company is going in or coming out.

Thursday 2nd December 3.40 pm

I was out last night setting a wiring party to work at about midnight. They also had a party out and we could hear them - and presumably they could hear us - but we all just got on with our wiring work.

I was lucky to get to 'A' this tour as we are fairly dry in our line and 'C' are in fact knee deep in mud all along their fire trench - and it's thick liquid mud.

I wonder if there will be a truce out here this Christmas like last year. I wonder if we will be allowed a truce this time - but I guess not.

Friday 3rd December 6.45 pm

There is a rumour that I am going to take over the transport for a time as Uthwaite who is in charge has gone back again. I am sorry he's gone as he's a good man for the job and likes it.

I saw John today and also Cyril. We have had one battalion of Tom's Division in with us so I hope he may come somewhere near soon.

Saturday 4th December 8.45 pm

I am away getting my teeth attended to - I have two with the stopping out so while we are out of the trenches I'm having them patched up.

I find Uthwaite is here and not gone back to the Base as envisaged. He hopes to be back with the Battalion in a few days. Ash is seeing to transport for the time being.

Cyril is with our HQ at present for a course of instruction so when I get back I hope to see a good amount of him.

We've had quite a merry evening. I am on the 3rd Field Ambulance and go back to the CCS tomorrow. This is a topping old house and makes quite a good hospital.

Sunday 5th December 6.50 pm

I am back at another hospital and my teeth are to be seen tomorrow. There is no one in here and only four others - officers - in the whole place at all. One is a

General who was hurt in a motor accident and there is a Lt. Col. deafened by a shell and two subalterns.

I had a topping ride here in front of an ambulance car and it was a grand sunny morning.

Monday 6th December 4 pm

I saw the dentist this morning. It took just ten minutes all told. He drilled and drilled and then dived about and came across a nerve which he poked and then announced 'exposed'. He put some stuff on and I am to go again tomorrow at 11.30 a.m.

It's quite comfortable here and there are nice nurses. We are not allowed out of here except to stroll to the dentist. I would soon believe I was sick if I stayed here too long though. They feed one up well and there is a hot water bottle in each bed which - I might add - I turned out as soon as I discovered it. I managed to drink the whisky and lemon.

One of the nurses is a 'Terrier' so we're good pals. I am now just going to see the other fellows who have to remain in bed. I haven't seen them all day.

Tuesday 7th December 8.15 pm

Right - well I have had the tooth stopped, the other two are being left as the dentist has far too many patients to deal with.

I will be off back to the Battalion tomorrow. I hope they do not keep me at the 3rd Field on the way for a night.

Thursday 9th December 9.15 pm

I understand that no leave at all is to be given for Christmas.

Friday 10th December 6.45 pm

I have just had a lovely hot bath. It was only a wee wooden tub with not very much water but it was still very pleasant.

I think I may get some leave in the New Year.

I guess the darned trenches will be in a fine state when we get in tomorrow. The weather is rotten.

Saturday 11th December 3.45 pm

I have just been for a walk around the trenches. The water did not come over my knees.

Monday 13th December 1 pm

There was a hard frost last evening. One keeps warm outside but the dugouts are so cold without a fire. Fuel is rather short just now so we do not light a fire before three or four o'clock.

I had a field postcard from Tom last night. I hear he may be fairly near and I am trying to find out. Cyril will not be too far away but as I am in the trenches I cannot get away.

Tuesday 14th December 2 pm

Glad to say I am just as fit as ever - in fact I have never felt better. I do not seem to feel the cold like some of the others do and I have not yet got all my full winter togs on.

Fuel is coming along better now. Things are very still around this area. We send a few shells over now and again and the reply with a few back but he does not send half as many our way as he used too. The frost is giving us a chance to clean up the trenches but a frost does more harm than good as a rule. It is the after effects that tell.

Wednesday 15th December 3.15 pm

We are not having too bad a time and there has been no rain for two days now. There was a frost though and a cold wind last night. 'C' company have the worse piece of line so I was lucky to get the change. 'A' is about the best at present. 'B' is good also but gets shelled most.

Shells have been flying around all morning to the Bosh. They sent three or four heavy 300 pounders in exchange. Ah - there goes another - that's one of ours - and yes - there goes another. That will make someone sit up, knocking the place well behind the front line.

I spent all the morning up in the front line, seeing to the pumping and also trying to find out just where the 'Minnies' were being despatched from, but they did not send another one while I was on look-out. You should see them. They are 3' 9" long and 9" wide and 300 lbs. in weight. That is a big 'Minnie'. A 'Little Minnie' is about half the length and 6" wide. They go up the deuce of a height, then gradually curve and then come down 'plump' followed by a bang and earth flies with pieces of shell. 'Minnie' is not popular!

Our enemy have little peace now - our guns are going every day and we send four to one if they fire. A 'Minnie' calls for a dozen or so assorted in return.

It is so very different to last winter - or even March this year - when we took over. The used to send us four to one then. You could not believe the difference in the last month or two.

At least it's cheery to hear our guns playing. One knows then that the Bosh would get hell if they attempted to rush us here.

Friday 17th December 4.50 pm

We've had some 'strafing' our guns today. The enemy sent in reply half a dozen very near here - one of them not five yards away. I was up on the front line at the time - it is the best place.

There is to be no 'truce' this year - we are ordered that when the enemy are seen they are to be shot and any man trying to be friendly appropriately dealt with.

Saturday 18th December 4.15 pm

There is to be some Christmas leave after all. Mason

and Coley are going so that should bring my turn a week closer.

Sunday 19th December 4.30 pm

I don't think I will see Cyril on the 25th as at present I learn he's some way from here - half an hour's walk or so.

I saw an air fight today. One of our planes drove two aeroplanes away, damaging one, right over our lines.

Monday 20th December 5.35 pm

Cyril has been in for tea today. I understand Coldicote is none too well. I hope he does not go all the way back to Blighty as then I will be left with the Company for a while longer. There is always a lot to do as OC and no extra pay - however it means for the time being I have a gee to call upon and that is good.

Tuesday 21st December 5.20 pm

It is a rotten day. I went for a walk to the transport this afternoon and got my knees horribly wet. Colonel Elton has sent each Company a brace of pheasant which is very decent of the old boy. We'd all love to see him back.

Coldicote has gone through to the CCS but I do not think he will get to England. A paragraph in orders last night stated 'Capt. H. R. Hoskins will take over the command and payment of 'A' company during Capt. Coldicote's absence in hospital.

Wednesday 22nd December 4 pm

We look like having a great Christmas. Tonight we are having a trial dinner and we have some fellows coming in. I believe the menu to be soup, fish, cakes, pheasant etc. and then plum pudding, sardines on toast, flavoured with Gentlemen's Relish. There will be cheese, coffee and cigars.

As for drinks - we shall have sherry, port and whiskey. We should do well.

I believe there will be plenty of sweets, fruit etc. and a Christmas tree with crackers.

The room is already a fair and beautiful sight. Music will be softly floating in from without! Some dinner for six!

I believe Cyril will be at HQ for Christmas. We are to ask him here one night before as we don't mean to get caught on Christmas Day. We're to have two dinners beforehand, then if we do get fetched on the 25th we'll be able to keep smiling.

I have some mistletoe from home with a number of toys for the tree. I've got it rigged up and it looks very fine.

Thursday 23rd December 4 pm

The dinner was a great success. It was a fine spread. The two attached officers, a Major and a Captain, were quite delighted. They tell us that their officers, NCOs and men have a real good opinion of the Warwicks. They are a north country brigade.

We have a good fire tonight of coal, coke and wood and it's the best we've had for some days. Really you would not think we are in the top of a place the Bosh could shell at any moment. We are all just as happy as 'fighting cocks'.

Friday 24th December 5.15 pm

Cyril and three of 'B' Company are coming to dinner. Unfortunately one of our chaps is feeling rotten and another is out on a working party which I take tomorrow. I shall be up in the front line on Christmas Eve for four hours and I shall be Orderly Officer tomorrow.

Sunday 26th December 1.50 pm (Boxing Day)

There was a concert for the men last night, which went with a good swing. We understood there was to be no post so you may guess how delighted I was to get back here about ten to see a pile of things for me and a parcel from home. Parcels have come along in fine style - I have had three or four most days this week.

We are off to the trenches tomorrow. They will be in a fine state as we have had any amount of rain. I am quite merry and bright and had quite a good Christmas and enjoyed these last few days.

There was a Service last night and a short address from the Padre. We also had a Communion Service, followed by the concert in the same barn. I will not attempt to describe all our doings this Christmas for I could write a book thereon.

Monday 27th December 4.45 pm

Three or four parcels received - from Dad, Uncle Jack and Hoskins & Sewell - all cigars, so I am very well set up in that line! Also a pair of topping gloves and the stockings I have been sent will be really useful. I will send postcards to all who have sent me parcels.

Our old friend 'Minnie' has been dropping around. I had one twenty yards or so away. I was well down in the trench so only got spattered with mud etc. I am well splashed also as I was in water up to my knees. There were half a dozen of us - the others thought it best to run. I felt safer staying where I was. No one was hurt. We have had eight within 100 yards - six I would say within 50 yards. Our fellows get rather fed up and it is so trying not being able to go for anyone. There would be a rough house if they were loose tonight.

Tuesday 28th December 4.15 pm

I hope to get leave next week but at this point it is not settled. There has been a lively cannonade this afternoon and a few more 'Minnies'. No damage to flesh and bone - only trenches.

Thursday 30th December 3.30 pm

Cyril has rung me up to say he'll be round for tea. I see quite a good amount of him now. He likes his job and it saves him going into the trenches for patrols etc.

Things in general are going A1. The detail in this trench warfare is tremendous.

Friday 31st December 4.30 pm

We have had a good shelling today but no damage. It is extraordinary how many shells can drop around without doing damage.

1916

Saturday 1st January, 1916 2.30 pm

I will know today if I am for leave this week. I will be seeing Cyril in a moment and perhaps he will have found out. I believe we get seven clear days in England now.

Ah - I hear I have got leave Tuesday next - so I guess I shall be home Thursday. I should be in London about midday.

Sunday 2nd January 11.55 am

I had a line from Coldicote yesterday. He has been very ill and only came off milk on the 31st so we will not be seeing him for some time.

It's a wretched day today - raining hard. Still it is about the first rain we've had this tour, so we've been lucky. The 1/8th had rain every day and heavy rain too.

On leave until Saturday 15th January, 1916

Departed Waterloo at 4 pm

Monday 17th January 4.30 am

Here I am again, well in the front. I've just been for a walk around the trenches and they appear to be in fine condition. I've seen the Colonel. He greeted me with 'Hallo little stranger, we're glad to see you back'!

Had a topping crossing and slept all the way. We got into a train this side at 3.30 am and arrive this end at 9.30 pm. I slept at the same cottage as before, had lunch at the transport and here we are - all merry and bright. I have seen Cyril and he is quite fit. There is no news of the much talk about 'rest' yet.

'Minnie' has been still of late I am told so I hope she'll remain so for a long time. Thirty six was the ration for one day while Cyril was in.

Tuesday 18th January 4.45 pm

The telephone folk have just been in to borrow the gramophone. They say they feel down in the dumps so I hope it will buck them up.

I seem to have heaps of letters to censor.

Saturday 22nd January 3.30 pm

I had lunch with Cyril today as I am on my own. One subaltern is away fetching a draught and the other away with our Battalion who are playing in the Divisional Cup Tie. I expect to be learning the half time score soon.

Hello, hello, hello. They are at it again. We've been sending them a few lumps of iron over and now they are returning them ('Thank you - that was near enough!')

Things are quite lively at present. The latest addition is a thing the throw in the trenches like an oil drum, filled with high explosive and odd pieces of iron, nails etc. A 'dud' one lay in our Communications trench as I came off patrol the other night. They are about 8" or 9" by 18" and weigh about 30 to 50 lbs. My man has just brought in a piece of these shells - it is an inch thick.

The Divisional Cup Tie - news just come is that we led at half time by one goal to nil. I hope they do not get shelled as they are only a short distance from the front line.

Result - 2 : 0.

Monday 24th January 1.50 pm

Yesterday I went along to transport and stayed for a cinema show in the village which was A1. All the company CO's are going to dinner with the Colonel tonight at 7.30. I expect he has a few words to spout as well.

Tuesday 25th January 4.30 pm

We had a fine show last evening. We had to Stand-To at 2 am and the guns were kicking up the deuce of a row. I really expected that we had got to stop a rush, but nothing doing. Then we were told to return to our billets and found out that they had paid a visit to the 1/8th - there was nothing much done. The 1/8th had two killed and two wounded, so we got off quite lightly as the shells were quite lively.

The Maxim bullets are flying over here and they ruin

our roof - I have had to have several tiles put on this morning.

We will I am afraid be having most of our officers suffering with nerves if we do not get a rest soon. The 8th will have to stop their 'bounce' about medals for the time now after last night. I cannot tell you more at the moment.

Wednesday 26th January 6.30 pm

We play against the 6th tomorrow in the Divisional Cup. I do hope we win as we shall be top of the Brigade then.

Thursday 27th January

I've been out watching the match against the 6th. It was great. No score so they played twenty minutes extra, ten each way, and we scored in the first ten and won so we are top of the Brigade. The next match is a semi-final for the Divisional Cup.

Friday 28th January 5 pm

I am glad to say we are in again for a while. I am really jolly glad to be in as we've had three alarms this last time out that fetched us out of bed.

Last night at about 7.00 there was a gas alarm and again this morning early. Both were false.

Things are looking up though - it is certainly getting hot on the line. We've heard heavy firing some way off on our left the last few days - some show on behalf of the French.

I am delighted we won the match yesterday - most folk expected the 1/6th to win. It has quite bucked up the Battalion and the footballers are being made as much of as possible - no front line jobs for them!

They must have heard us cheering yesterday quite distinctly. I wonder what they took it to be.

Saturday 29th January 4.20 pm

I had an interesting stroll this morning at about 4.20 am for an hour or so. I went right up to the wire and had a general look around. We were not fired upon.

Sunday 30th January 2.10 pm

Some of our Division went into the trenches last evening so that helps to square things up a little - I haven't heard with what result. It is very foggy here and has been all last evening and today.

I had a line from Tom last night. He tells me that his Battalion has got measles so they will all be kept out of the trenches for a while I expect.

The great thing now is gas. Everyone imagines they are being gassed - it is very annoying. A man last night thought he was gassed and really it was only the concussion from a shell that had dropped near.

One of the chaps has gone to hospital for a few days with trench fever. It is just from the cold and he is generally run down through strain of it all.

My wee white kitten is dead - it must have picked up some poison.

Oh well - I have a fine fire in here and I am as warm as toast. There is plenty of fog about so I am allowed it.

Monday 31st January 4.15 pm

I am due in the trenches at 4.30 pm, My next two patrols are 4.30 to 8 and 5 am to 8 am. We are only three officers now, so we have to do extra time. Things have quietened down again some today, but the guns are booming away all day up north of the country.

Tuesday 1st February, 1916 4.20 pm

Officers play in the Division football if good enough but it is Association football not Rugby. No officers played in the 1/7th v 1/6th.

I was on patrol last evening and had the enemy transport shelled, also a wiring party fired upon who dispersed to cries of 'Hoch, Hoch'. Then I was on again at 2 am and about 5 am a German patrol managed to get into our wire near a Lewis gun and we made them get off at the double. I sent out a patrol and found they'd left a rifle and a glove.

Most of the day we've been shelling and we are going out early in case they think of fetching the rifle!

Fancy it being February - we shall soon have been out here a year.

Wednesday 2nd February 4.15 pm

I am up in the front line dugout as I am on patrol from

12-5 this afternoon. I spent from 6-7 last evening out in front with some men looking for the enemy, but when they began wiring we knew we'd not see any patrols of theirs so I came in while they had a look along the wire.

We want to get a Bosh, dead or alive, to see who is in front of us. We should have had one or two the other night if there had been two good men on one post, but they spoilt our fun by getting windy and shooting too soon, so giving the patrol warning.

The bombardment up north seems to have started again today. Looks like they are beginning the 'grand attack' we've heard of so often.

Friday February 4th 3.30 pm

They are putting a few shells in the village today - I hear five have been wounded - one man of ours and four of the 1/5th.

The weather has broken up. It began to rain about 3.15 am when I was on patrol.

Saturday 5th February 1.30 am

I am up on patrol and it's a dark wet night, so dark that one keeps walking into pools of water and tumbling off the trench boards. The Zeppelin raid should do any amount of good and bring the warning home to some of those folk who haven't been able to get the idea!

I am now in the signallers' dugout having just had a tour round the sentries and found 'all correct'.

Night Rounds in the trenches

Monday 7th February 7 pm

I have returned from the 'pictures' and it was quite a good show and passed an hour or so away very well. The 'cinema' is an old barn converted and a good job they've made of it too.

We play the semi-final for the 'Fanshaw Cup' on Thursday. It will create some excitement that day and it is to be hoped we win.

Tuesday 8th February 4.20 pm

We've had a supper party on tonight. We shall be a table of twelve instead of the usual three in the Company Mess.

I have just returned from a spin on Dick. It has done me good to have a ride even if I did get completely wet through.

Wednesday 9th February 1 pm

We have had a fall of snow early this morning but the sun has cleared it all away now and it's a fine day, cold and fresh with any amount of mud.

Cruggins has just been in to see if everything is fixed up for the match tomorrow. The 8th I hear have had a few men knocked out. They were well back in the village too - just walked outside their billet and were killed by a machine gun bullet. That village of ours is becoming quite a warm corner. I always say the Front Line is the safest place.

Some news today. Major Hake is to arrive in a day or so and he is to have this Company as I am the junior Captain in charge of a Company. We are not jumping for joy. One of our chaps gives him a month before he cracks up - he has not met 'Minnie' yet.

Ah - the big match sets off tomorrow at 2.30 pm.

We enjoyed a great dinner last evening - twelve strong and afterwards we had all the officers in here. We went to the pictures and tonight we have 'The Varletts' - they are the 1st Field Ambulance troupe. I am going to 'C' company afterwards for supper.

Taking everything together we are having a good time and most of the men are on working parties etc. so that the officers are having quite a good rest. They like being here too and have become used to the few hours on working parties and know if they were not on that they'd have to be on parades instead. They do not have to work too hard on the jobs they get.

Thursday 10th February 9.30 pm

The Match was a draw - one all - after twenty minutes extra time. We had the Divisional Band here this evening and jolly good it was too.

Friday 11th February 4.30 pm

I went to the 'Orphuls' last night. They are our own Brigade Pierrot Troup and it was a great show.

I have quite enjoyed this week out of the trenches and feel fitter for it.

I haven't seen Cyril for some time. He comes here tomorrow so I hope we meet up.

Saturday 12th February 8.40 pm

It will not matter telling you now but the last time just before we went into the trenches we were told there would be a show. To cut it short, I was to take several men out with me to bomb. It would have been a fine chance to do something - only it was all cancelled. I was very bucked up at being picked for the job. Murray is Bomb Officer so he'd have to go but anyone might have been picked for my job.

I am just off for a tub soon - at least half a one. I could just do with a warm bath. I only get one every ten days at present.

Tuesday 15th February 6.15 pm

The match has gone against us this time so we are out of the final.

Wednesday 16th February 12.40 am

Ye gods - we are having a time in the trenches. It has rained for 48 hours and is still at it. We are in some new trenches, just to our left and they are above knee deep in mud for the most part. No dugout - just rough shelters. Quite the worst line we've struck yet. Some of 'Kitchener's' men have been here for some time - enough said!

The men are having a very rough time but keeping quite merry and bright. They do stick it wonderfully well. There is always the pleasure of knowing the Bosh must have their front line in a much worse state, as they are below us.

We have just had 'Hail, smiling morn' on the gramophone. It made us smile.

Thursday 17th February 2.15 pm

The rain cleared away last night and today is A1 and we are able to make some headway. In fact we've got these darned trenches almost dry.

Had one man killed today and two just wounded by shell fire - that makes three stretcher bearers hit out of our company just this last week.

Friday 18th February 5.20 pm

Had a stand-to about 2 o'clock this morning so I was on till about 3 pm when I went to bed and got in two good hours sleep.

The rain began about 10 am and still continues so the front line will be in a nice state again.

We had a night last night - one killed and five wounded so that makes nine casualties in two days.

Sunday 20th February 6 pm

We have all suffered a pretty rough tour this time. I've done about six hours already today and have three more to do.

Hake is off to the CCS tomorrow to have his hand X-rayed. He sprained it a few weeks ago and has taken a spill or two in the trenches which has upset his wrist.

Monday 21st February

I have a cold coming on tonight. I hope to get on top of it during the next few nights as I have no night work to do.

Thursday 24th February 3.20 pm

Snow is here, although no more has fallen since last night. My chill has greatly improved.

Friday 25th February 3.30 pm

It is really a dreadful day today and the snow is still here, quite a blizzard and it must be rotten for the men on the front line. I was out this morning and have never been out in such snow. There is one good thing about the snow and that is it stops work for the men and therefore a good amount of us as well.

I hear our old friend Minnie has come back opposite us and has sent a few messages across last evening. She's had a good holiday as we've not seen her for several weeks.

Saturday 26th February 12.50 pm

The snow is beginning to melt so there's a chance it will be gone before we go into the trenches again. No signs of leave being started again - I hope it will next week or you will all be disappointed.

One of the chaps is off on a twelve-day course tomorrow so that leaves me on my own. As we do not have much to do at present it will not make too much difference and I'll be given one or two for the trenches.

I have received the wire and letters tell me Dad is very ill. Since I had Kath's letter I was afraid it might be so. I am afraid I shall be unable to get away. All leave is cancelled and we are very low in officers. I have sent a message to the Colonel and I will do all I can to get home to you.

Grand Hotel de la Poste
Thursday March 9th 1916

I have only got halfway back at present. This is a topping hotel and a week or so here would do me a lot of good.

We had a splendid crossing. I haven't seen Tom since Waterloo.

Saturday 11th March 6.10 pm

We reached here last night at 9 pm and we should not have been here until this morning if a cart had not been at the station for Captain Lang. He is attached to this Company for instruction and will take command of it when he's got hold of the idea.

They have had a rotten time of it in the trenches last tour - quite the worst they have experienced.

We are quite flush with officers now; a few of those who were sick have now returned.

Sunday 12th March 6.15 pm

News of Dad's death came this afternoon. Cyril had his wire first and then came to see me.

I shall not be able to get away again. I saw the Colonel and he told me to go and see the Brigadier, but he says it is quite useless to put in for leave as we have one brother still at home.

Wednesday 15th March 2.35 pm

We had a Battalion show this morning and there is a lecture at 6 pm, after which I am going to the Transport for supper.

The Order regarding Captains going in front has again come out and is to be implemented. No Captain is go in front save for a special purpose, so I'll be losing my bit of fun.

I am just going to try and relax by watching the platoons play footer Also I believe the Battalion is playing the RAMC.

Saturday 18th March 3.15 pm

I have just about got my trench legs again now. We had some near ones last night up in the trench and those oil drums I've talked about were flying around bursting in the air and all about us as we were coming down. I had Lang with me. He'd got a pair of trench boots on and kept slipping over. I could have been under cover if I'd been alone but I couldn't leave the old boy on his own. Still no one was hurt so it's all right.

Sunday 19th March 2.40 pm

Leave is on again so I expect John is on his way home.

The party on leave left last evening. They just missed a further 'strafe'.

I was on patrol at 11.30 to 2.30 and at about 1.30 I was wondering how long the hour would take to pass when the guns began, so out I popped to find it was away on our right and we were getting the edge of it. So I got our guns going and we had a great time for an hour or so. Luckily they had heaps of duds on us and no one in the front line was hurt.

One fellow behind in my Company was killed. We are having a bad time - that makes two killed and four wounded this tour already. Poor old 'A' are having all the casualties of late. The men were all quite ready for Herr had he cared to show himself. So the hour passed in quick time - in fact I was not relieved until 3.45 am

The Bosh must have had a rotten time as we fairly blasted them with all kinds of shells and we'd given them a blasting earlier in the evening as they'd been too cheeky of late, so we gave them a double dose.

Tuesday 21st March 3.20 am

Lang - whom we call 'Flapper' - is not to have the Company yet. I have to give a report on him to the Colonel soon and say if I think he is fit to take over the Company. I certainly do not think so at present. No one can learn the whole game in a week and has to be smart to do so in four!

Wednesday 22nd March 4 pm

Up to now we have had quite a good innings this tour - much less strain on us all than it has been. The fine and warmer weather and the lighter days make a big improvement. We only have darkness from 6.45 pm to 5 am now - its great. It almost halves the work. I really believe there is a chance of us getting a rest soon and we deserve it.

Friday 24th March 5.45 pm

We have been very busy of late. There will probably be a note in the paper soon. The 8th went in this time and we had to sit tight in the front line and stick the shelling, which resulted in several casualties.

The old Company had three killed and about fifteen wounded last tour. We have had all the bad luck of late. The men are sticking it very well indeed.

I had two men on sentry duty get knocked off the fire step twice by bursting shells and they got back again. Another stood up and fired his pop-gun all the time the shells were dropping all around the place.

I was safe enough well back in the dugout. The 2nd in command had to be in the front line.

Sunday March 26th 3.10 pm

Yesterday I went for a joy-ride with Graham. He went to draw cash. We rode to a town a few miles back and had lunch there, followed by coffee etc. at a nice place where the daughter of the house is 19 and speaks broken English. She is one of the neatest girls I have seen so near the line.

We remained there until 4.30 and quite a nice afternoon and promised to go again about Thursday when I am to give the young lady another English lesson.

A & B Companies are together this time out so we are quite a lively mess and have good quarters.

Monday 27th March 3 pm

Cyril came in last night to say he was returning to his Company. Some row with the Brigadier made out - and Innes (although he knew Cyril was not to blame) would not stand up to the Brigadier for him.

'Flapper' as the old man is called is now trying to get back to the 2/8th. The Colonel told me today that he does not intend to keep him here. Anyway, he's not to have the Company.

Thursday 30th March 1.25 am

I am off with Graham for our joy-ride and for my next English lesson.

Friday 31st March 2.25 pm

Shelling is a little livelier of late, getting hot ready for our tour in. The 8th have had a soft time. I think we are changing trenches. 'D' and 'C' are to take 'A' and 'B' trenches as the latter have been getting all the strafing.

We had a merry afternoon yesterday. It did me good to get away and have a decent ride. The Colonel and the Major want to know what the attraction is at that town as four of us have been twice this week. The place is not an 'estaminet' *(Bistro)* but a respectable wine merchants so we are sort of guests. Only a few favoured ones can get anything, except wholesale.

Madam is a dear.

Saturday April 1st 4.10 pm

It's a wonder I am not in hospital, as a shell dropped within a few feet of me just about 1 pm. It wounded three and one I am afraid is bad. A tiny bit hit me but made only a tiny scratch by my ear. I do not wish to see one burst any closer and am not particular about them being so near. As a matter of fact there were two shells, both anti-aircraft shells badly timed. Very unfortunate for poor old 'A' Company.

Sunday 2nd April 3.10 pm

'A' Company is not so bad this tour. We've swapped over to the other side and we are out of the shelling a bit. The men stick it all right. Some - but not many - get very windy but they all say that if the shell has got your number on it, it'll get you.

I do not like this dugout as much as my old HQ, although it is further back. It is not nearly as comfortable - but for the shelling this is far and away the better position.

Monday 3rd April 3.45 pm

Our old pal Minnie has returned since the raid and is giving us heaps of iron. She blew in a dugout of 'B' company last night and buried several men. They dug one man out, who had only his head showing and heavy timber across his chest.

The first question one always asks is, is it one of 'ours' or not?

I am off for a walk up to the front line shortly as I have not been up there today yet. it's a deuce of a way from here and takes quite an effort.

Tuesday 4th April 2 pm

I have been up since 2.30 am so I am quite ready for a snooze. Things have gone quiet again now. Minnie did not trouble us last night. I am on patrol from about 9.30 to 11 pm.

Thursday 6th April 3.35 pm

I have a German paper here - dropped by an aircraft the other day. I am trying to find someone to translate it.

Sunday 9th April 4 pm

Graham is off to the hospital for a while - the place where I went for my teeth. Old Hanson is getting ready for a hot bath but an old woman keeps popping into his room. He is trying to devise some scheme to get her out of the way for a few minutes - its very funny!

Wednesday 12th April 5.20 pm

Yesterday I was out all day from 10 and rode about eighteen miles. It rained most of the time but I was well wrapped up and did not get too wet.

I have to be inoculated again tomorrow - all of us who haven't been done for twelve months. It can make some of the fellows quite bad so I hope I escape as before with just a stiff arm for a while.

Friday 14th April 5.10 pm

Yes - got the stiff arm but I have had a day off on the strength of it.

All leave has been stopped indefinitely now. I am just off to hear the Divisional Band play.

Saturday 15th April 1.20 pm

I had a topping ride to the village with no rain and plenty of sun. I broke a glass and Marie said it was good luck to them so I hope they do well.

It is becoming quite the place for the officers of the Battalion to ride out to.

I have also been out for a route march today. We were caught several times in hail and rain but were all dry before we got back.

Sunday 16th 1.45 pm

It is a splendid day with glorious sun and no wind and

I enjoyed a splendid ride with Bushel, Murray and some others. We went to see Marie again and left there about 5 pm, arriving back at 6 pm. Then we went to the 'Orphuls' which was a really good show. After that I went to Ash and Jones' place for dinner so it was not a bad day before going back into the trenches. I also attended a service today and stayed for communion.

Tuesday 18th April 3.15 pm

The trenches are getting wet – it's been raining since 4 am. A real beast of a day - heavy showers that drench everybody and everything. Hopefully it is just the last of the winter.

Easter Sunday 23rd April, 1916 2 pm

The weather has improved - at least we have not had rain since about 1 am and the sun has been out most of the day. The trenches are drying out again. That's one good thing about these trenches - they dry up almost as quickly as they get wet.

I have a man back with me for instruction but I hardly expect him to stick it for long as he jumps half a mile or so every time a shell pops off.

Thursday 27th April 4 pm

Ye Gods - its hot! A great change from last week - we seem to have gone bang straight into mid-summer. I went over to see Marie the day before yesterday. Her young sister who is eighteen months younger and her half-brother were there, so we had quite a party.

Friday 28th April 2.40 pm

Once again I am deposed from Company Commander and another man has taken my place. I'll soon be used to all these changes but it's rather depressing to have a fellow who has been in England for nine or ten months come out and take one's Company even if he is senior. I could have gone sick two or three times. Oh well! I guess we will have to put up with it.

Once we are back into the trenches he'll most probably crack up. Next time I will tell the Major I shall not take it on again unless I've got it for good and all as long as I am forced to be here.

I lose Dick as the new man cannot ride him. Still while we are here I will be able to have him when I like. I am really fed up and wish I'd been put second to Hanson.

Saturday 29th April 7.15 am

I am off for a route march - not on my feet thank you! As it happens the Company Officers are on another job so we 2nd in command have to take the march and those who can get gees. I've got Dick.

Sunday 30th April 12.45 pm

I gave Marie another English lesson today and I am trying to get her to pronounce the English 'h'.

Monday 1st May 8.45 pm

I am feeling slack as we paraded at 7.45 am and were out until 12.30 and again from 2 to 4 pm. During the morning all dismounted officers had to carry packs etc so I was a proper Christmas tree. It's the first time I have had my pack on and it was a bit warm.

I have been on the go all day. After tea I was about seeing billets and getting togs etc together for the men. I shall get to bed as soon as parade is at 7.20 in the morning and that means rising at 6.30 to get shaved and bathed.

I am not at all keen on this foot work I have to do now and I shall be glad when we get back to the trenches.

Thursday 4th May

Greg has been trying to tell me about the wonderful things that happened at the first place they went into in the trenches!!! He went back in June and was in hospital half the time before. Angus Greg is with a flying crew who often fly over us, as Observer.

Friday 5th May 3 pm

We are going to get a new Brigadier but I do not know his name. I think Knox will probably have this Battalion and Hanson will be Major.

Hanson's gang was a good company and I do not want to leave 'A' even for a couple of weeks.

The guns are booming away and keep it up pretty well.

Cyril is having a good long tour in the trenches. He's been in about twelve days or so.

Thursday 11th May 2 pm

I have had no mail for a day or two. I did have a line from Graham a few days ago. He is in St. Thomas' Hospital, London and none too well. He's been there about a fortnight.

Hanson is CO for a few days. He has his Major's stripes and I am jolly glad. He deserves them. Knox is now Colonel and I believe gets this Battalion. The new Brigadier has not arrived to date. I think now it will be a Colonel. Dent - a topping man.

Saturday 13th May 10.30 am

I am in the same village as John now. The reason why I have said nothing to home is that we are informed a great amount of news is getting through and that officers are the worst offenders. In future we will be court-martialled for writing news of moves and destinations etc. The Censor Department is getting rather annoyed, so it is wise to be careful.

We have a good mess room and sleep in a barn at present so we are quite OK.

I am going to play Rugby today for 'B' versus 'A'* but unless the weather improves some we may have to cancel the match.

* FOOTNOTE: It is probably here that Captain Hoskins damaged his knee, which necessitated a return home for a short period with a dislocated cartilage in the kneecap.

We are having a slack time just now - in fact one hardly knows what to do to pass the time. I am just taking life 'at ease' while I have the chance.

The folk here in the mess are very decent and we get on together very well. They treat us as we treat them.

There is a wee maid of seven here with whom I am great pals.

Sunday 14th May 12.10 pm

We held our rugby match in the rain last evening. 'A' company won by three points but 'B' were four men short in the team. It was a very jolly game.

We had church parade this morning in the open - the first for some time. At present I have a real bed and clean sheets at our mess - marvellous!

Cyril was in for supper last night but I haven't seen Leslie to speak to of late. I did spy him yesterday riding though.

Monday 15th/16th May

I believe the CO is in England now and not likely to return. Knox I should say is a better Second than CO but we shall see.

I am going round to Cyril's mess for supper - it is some time since I had a meal there.

Rock Shaw was near here the other day and was apparently asking for me. He was on his way for leave and I am sorry I missed him.

Left to right: Cyril Hoskins, 1st/8th Batt. RW Regt; Captain Hoskins, 1st/7th Batt. Royal Warwickshire Regt; Private Tommy Hoskins, 14th Batt. RW R; Lt. Peter Hoskins, 3rd/8th Batt. RW Regt.

I had a photo of us four yesterday - it is quite good and will be worth having in - say - ten or twenty years.

Wednesday 17th May 9.40 am

We parade at 6.40 am tomorrow for a route march so as to get the cool of the day and it looks as if it will be hot again like today. I must have ridden over 20 miles today so I am well tired and ready for bed.

Thursday 18th May 10.30 pm

We were up at 5 am and undertook a long march,

getting in about 12.30 pm. As usual the 7th had no men fall out on the way - our men march splendidly.

Greg is back and also Mason and as 'A' and 'B' are messing together we have the pleasure of all being together all the time. I hope to get away on a month's course at some point.

The new Brigadier has shown up at last and I should say by the look of him he will make a useful man.

Cyril's mess is quite close so I went round to see him this evening. He is still Company OC and has been since one of the men got hit.

Saturday 21st May 2.30 pm

Well it does not look as if I shall get home again just yet. Colonel Knox does not seem keen for me to again yet except for the 'special' leave.

Actually I don't see why I should be put back and I cannot count on getting away for the special course either yet.

Last Post is just sounding, which means someone is to be buried.

6.15 pm

I have just learned that I am for the course leave some time next week which will be a pleasant change for a bit. I also believe John is going on the same course.

Sunday 22nd May 11.20 am

I have just returned from church parade, which was a good show with the Divisional Band in attendance, so I am off for a swim for a few moments. It should be champion - I like these days when the sun is hot early in the day. I always wash outside and have a proper swill down.

John was on parade but I had no chance of a word with him so I must pop in to see him later.

Tuesday 23rd May 4.15 pm

We have been out all day and had lunch out. The roads are very dusty and we usually return almost white from head to foot.

I am off to 'school' on Sunday for a month. John is hoping to be with me but he is at present not quite sure.

Leave is off again for a short time but I was not expecting to get home until the month's course is over. With luck I will get home straight from there.

Thursday 25th May 7 pm

I am seated on the floor in a hut. We had a fairly long route march early this morning and I am tired in my feet. It rained cats and dogs most of the way. I hope it carries on tomorrow, then we'll march back instead of having a field day. Still - 'Jolly Old War' - it will not last for ever!

The heavy guns are going just now to remind me that there is really a show on not very far away.

I think I will sleep tonight. We were up at 1.30 am. I was not in bed before 11.30, so I shall get down soon after supper. I have to be up again at 3 am for early parade. 'Jolly Old War'.

Oh - drat it - they say we shall not get any post until we get back on Saturday.

Sunday 28th May 3.45 am

So here I am back at school again. I arrived about 11 pm and have a good billet and mess. There are seventeen of us in the mess but at this point I cannot say yet if they are a jolly gang or not. John DID come along with me and this course will take a little flesh off him. It can't take anything off me as I'm too fit for extra flesh!

Monday 29th May 5.15 pm

John is in No. 3 syndicate and I am in No. 4, which of course looks like being the best. My mess is No. 6 and its not too bad and I think we'll be able to shake things up some just now. There are two fellows in this billet with me and we have shaken down together and everything seems OK up to date.

This is an Officers' Training Course - 150 of us and also 150 NCOs. We begin at the very bottom with drill and all the things a recruit goes through. It is great on parade to see a frosty old fellow turning smartly left instead of right. I really think it looks like being a jolly old 28 days.

I am told we are going to have that Daylight Saving game out here.

Wednesday 31st May 5 pm

We have had quite a busy day. First parade was at 7 am. It is good to see a company of officers marching along with rifles and there is plenty of fun for those who see it.

There is a show on tonight by the 'Wiz-bands' at 8.30 pm I hope they are good.

We are all in different syndicates here. They put one from each Brigade in each syndicate so it splits us all up.

Friday 2nd June 1916 7.10 pm

I enjoyed a topping swim today. We have the Commandant and Adjutant of the School in for dinner this evening. The Commandant is a topping fellow and just the man for the job.

I must say I am having a jolly good time and I shall have even a better one when the mess gets really on the go. I can see I will have to take things in hand unless matters improve. I was trying to keep out of it because I wanted a rest from the mess department.

This Course is pulling me together in fine style - it gets one's fighting spirits up fresh and alive again. No one can do all the trench work we have to do and not lose - quite without realising it - the top notch.

Tuesday 3rd June 5 pm

I was off for the whole day yesterday. We were on the go all day. Drill from 7-8 am. We practised an attack from 9.30-1 p.m. Then there was a bayonet drill and a lecture followed by dinner at 8 pm. I was jolly glad to get bed after all that.

Our mess is ten to fifteen minutes away from the parade ground but we have the use of a bus as a rule.

Today we were on parade again at 9.30 and then went out to carry out a scheme and got absolutely drenched in the rain. There is a lecture again this evening at 6 pm. It will be an early parade again tomorrow and much the same programme so we are kept at it pretty well.

No. 4 is bucking up and No. 6 mess is not too bad.

Bayonet practice - British training

Thursday 6th June 5 pm

Your Humble is going along fine and enjoying a splendid time altogether. I am learning a good deal and there is plenty of hard work. We are on the hop all day and in a moment I have to rush off for another lecture.

It is extraordinary how little time one gets to write home. This is the first chance I have had today and I shall not get another chance to sit and write as it is a Guest Night and we have our Major and Captain coming in. There is sure to be plenty of fun.

Friday 9th June 5.10 pm

Its been another long day with drill from 7-8 am and after breakfast an engineering lecture and demonstration. Then there is some jolly old bayonet fighting this afternoon. Bayonet fighting is really great. One has to put all one's vim and vigour into every movement - I like it. Some are making a fuss over it but why I don't know as every man needs to be able to use a bayonet and learn to be quick with it also.

Sunday 11th June 10.45 pm

Two weeks have passed here already and it seems no time at all. It is undoubtedly doing me a lot of good and I am full of life and vigour. I thought I might get a morning in bed today but I got up at 9.30 and am just off for the day now. I hope to get back about 10 pm

Monday 12th June 9.55 pm

We had an early parade today at 7 am and have been at it all day including riding school this afternoon which I quite enjoyed. There is to be an early parade tomorrow also.

I saw John to speak to today and he hopes to get some leave after this course. I have written about it and am now awaiting a reply.

Tuesday 13th June

Things are livening up now everywhere. We are not putting black armlets on out here for Kitchener. The Order I understand only applies to officers at home.

I believe the syndicate is to be photographed one day soon and I will send a copy if we do have a picture taken. They are a jolly set of fellows.

Thursday 15th June 9.30 am

Daylight saving commenced last evening, hence it is still daylight. Last evening a few of us were in the mess at 10.40 pm and we put our watches on and behold - it was 11.40 and as all messes close - or should do - at 11 pm we were breaking the rules!

No news as yet about some leave.

Friday 16th June 9.40 pm

I have a line about leave now. It says I can take some

leave following the course - that will be about Tuesday week. It's not certain of course. It may be stopped.

Monday 19th June 6 pm

No more word about leave. I only know that I shall have to go back to the Battalion first. We are due to depart from here on Sunday - early.

My word, this month has gone fast - it seems no time since we arrived. It has been a topping month and even with all the work it has been quite a good rest, for I have only heard the rumble of a gun once or twice the whole time.

Captain Bushill is in England. He has three months' leave to look after the works as his governor is away very ill. He was mentioned in despatches a day or two ago. We shall miss him as there are jolly few of the old crew left now.

We had a topping concert on Saturday night by the 'Tykes' - a really first class show and very well staged. Quite the best show I've seen out here up to date.

Wednesday 21st June 2 pm

Bad news about Rock Shaw. I'll be having a score up against 'Mr. Bosh' soon. Let's hope I get a chance to wipe some of them out - I will be very annoyed if I get wounded or invalided back now without getting a chance of a smack at him.

We had a grenade lecture this morning and I feel bomb mad!

I have managed to put in a few extra hours at bayonet

fighting. We have several competitions this week and I'm involved in it all of course. It is mostly teams of eight or more. There is only one individual show and that's the Bayonet Fight. I am not sure if I will be in that as there are only four from each syndicate.

I am off now to do some map reading etc.

Thursday 22nd June 9.10 pm

There is no news of leave being stopped at this point so I am still living in hope. We had a photo taken today and I hope it turns out ok.

Lawks! Another early parade tomorrow. We had one today and also the bayonet competition tomorrow. Time is nearly up now I am sorry to say. I could do with another week or two here.

Friday 23rd June 6.30 pm

I got my wish - the Course has been extended, but of course it means I will not be able to take leave.

My gang (No. 4) won the Syndicate Bayonet Competition today. We were top of all eight syndicates so that is better - we were bottom in drill yesterday!

Tomorrow we have wiring. The officers have whacked the NCOs each time up to now and I hope we shall tomorrow also to complete things. The NCOs should have done better in drill and bayonet work as they have done so much more than we have and had the same training.

We have been warned again about keeping everything

'mum' when writing home etc and told that two officers and twelve men are at this moment on the carpet. A single postcard found on a raid in the trenches gave no less than five very important pieces of information to our intelligence folk. See how easy it is!

We had a good lecture by a fellow who was in all the fighting at the beginning. He was one of three who kept about a hundred at bay and turned them back by the way they had come. He's the sort of man you can really listen to and learn from.

Saturday 24th June 8 pm

I am having an afternoon off altogether and I guess I'll go to sleep before long. The competitions have all finished, with no more parades for the present and I will not being going out on a joy trip today.

The weather is very unsettled. We keep getting very heavy showers between sunshine but it is much warmer the last few days.

Monday 26th June 9.20 pm

We went for a route march this morning and had lunch out. We are to do all schemes on foot, walking to the places instead of going in a bus. Tomorrow I see we are to parade in full marching order and packs, so we are getting a stiffish time this week.

There was a good lecture tonight on the reasons and causes leading up to the war. It continues tomorrow. A good lecture and very well presented.

Friday 30th June 1.30 pm

We are to have a School Sports Day today. I seem to be entering everything of course although I was never much good but its all in the day's fun.

We won the officers' syndicate tug-of-war yesterday. I did not expect that, as No. 3 are much heavier.

Saturday July 1st 1916 3.15 pm

We finished up yesterday easily top of all syndicates by thirteen marks. I was fagged out at the end and my knees are still shaky. It certainly stirred up a few parts that had not been in use of late!

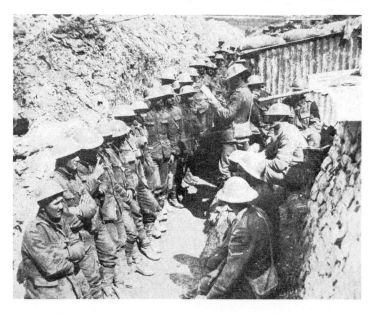

Roll Call in the Trenches, 1st July 1916

Letter to home to Mother with the news of Cyril's death

July 5ᵗʰ 1916

My dear Mother,

I am now back with the Battalion, and only yesterday knew that Cyril had been killed. I expect you will know before you get this letter. I have seen several of the 8ᵗʰ fellows, and all are loud in their praise of his deeds and tell me he was fine. It was a day of many fine deeds and for anyone to stand out particularly must have done remarkably well; Cyril did that.

I'll just tell you shortly what happened. The 8ᵗʰ had to take the first, second and third lines of Bosh trenches. The guns were supposed to put all machine guns out of action, but for various reasons as events proved, failed to do so, the result being that as soon as the 8th got out of their trenches they were met by heavy fire, and no one knows what machine gun fire is who has not been under it. Well, Cyril walked along the parapet on top and rallied his Company, got them out and formed up in line, and then advanced towards the Bosh first line. He was already hit in the shoulder, but pistol in hand he took his men ahead. He got another wound, but kept ahead. It was at the third line as he was aiming at a Bosh that he was shot dead.

You can be assured he suffered no pain and died a glorious death, leaving nothing but praise and admiration behind for the wonderful way he led his

Company. This also shows up when I tell you that only two out of the four Companies got out at the appointed time. The 5th and 6th did wonderful work and everyone is saying so.

I am distressed at losing him, but so proud he proved his worth and died not only doing his duty but doing it so wonderfully well. I have talked with some of his men who were near and they are as proud of him. His body will be where he fell, as the Bosh retook all the ground.

I am going to look through his kit, and send some home. There is a rush to catch the post now so I'll write again. Do not be downhearted, as it would not be fair to his memory; you should feel proud at his leadership. He is the first Hoskins to fall, and fell covered in glory.

Friday 7th July 10.30 am
(Letter home)

I know what a shock it will have been to you to know that Cyril has been killed - and Brian and all the others too. I wrote to Mother yesterday. I did not know anything about it until I had returned here.

Copper Murray is also killed - a direct hit with a shell while walking around the trenches. Eric M. is very down. He is really badly upset and I am doing all I can to cheer him up as it is bad for him and his work.

We have decided that we are not going to put on black armlets. They have rather a depressing effect on folk. One can never feel real lively when the fellow next to you has one.

Cyril died as glorious a death as any man could - doing his duty to such an extent that he has drawn praise from all directions. I told Mother that on a day of so many grand deeds for any one man to shine in particular, he must have dome some wonderful work - Cyril did that.

At 7.30 am Cyril had orders to take his Company (B) over the parapet and take four lines of German trenches - others having the same orders on each side.

At 7.25 the machine guns opened fire but nothing dismayed, at the given hour up jumps Cyril and walks along the parapet calling his men out. No one who has not been under machine gun fire knows what that is like and what it meant. He got his men out and lined up and started to walk across 'No Man's Land' to the front line. He was, I am told, already shot in the left shoulder. His Company took or put out of action a few machine guns and so on to the third line of trenches. Cyril - I am told - having shot a few on the way, all the time cheered his men along and kept perfect control (a task that requires long training and strength of mind). The men must have had every confidence in him. In fact since I've spoken to some of them they cannot say enough - Cyril was very popular and a first class officer.

He was hit again before he fell - it was at the third line - he was just about to use his revolver when a shot fetched him down. I understand he was not seen to move again.

You cannot picture a more glorious charge and death than that - the 8th and 6th have covered themselves in glory.

The 8th got the 4th line with two companies - Cyril's was one.

Enclosed is a postcard* of him with his Company officers and NCOs taken about a month ago. I am sending a larger one* home with also a group of the 8th officers. All save three have been killed or wounded.

You will be proud to know that our Brigade made the finest show around this part of the line. My Battalion and the 1/5th were in some other trenches all the time and came out with less casualties.

I am so sad at losing my brother Cyril - yet proud - so very proud of him.

*FOOTNOTE Unfortunately these postcards cannot be found.

Saturday 18th July

I am off on working party at 1 pm Yesterday it rained all day hard and all last evening too, so today it is all mud and slush everywhere but so far the weather is keeping fine - in fact quite hot.

I am now with 'B' Company in charge so now I've been to every company as O.C. We are in bivies now (bivouacs) which is rather a change to the way in which I have been living of late. I have six officers besides myself.

Oh - I've been out for a spin on old Dick - it was wonderful to be on his back again.

Original of letter from
J. C. Wilson – text below

Headquarters 8
1/8 R. War. Reg.
B.E.F.
17th July, '16

Dear Capt. Hoskins

I have been waiting before writing to you in the hope of hearing something definite about what happened to your brother, Lt. Hoskins, on 1st of July.

All I can hear from any of the NCOs or men at present with the Battalion is that Lt. Hoskins when gallantly leading his Company in the attack was wounded - it is feared mortally - about the German second line.

This loss is a very serious one to the Battalion. How much more to yourself! I can only assure you that the few original officers left with the Battalion, including myself, offer to you our deepest sympathy.

It is hardly necessary to add that whatever work Lieut. Hoskins undertook was thoroughly well done and the only consolation I can offer to you is that he died like a true patriot for his King and Country.

Yours sincerely, J. C. Wilson - Charge Captain Commanding 1/8th R. War. Reg.

Monday 17th July 7.25 pm

Home will see by the papers that we've been in it again. The guns all around me are kicking up the deuce of a row. We have been sitting in this field this afternoon watching a few shells bursting across the road, perhaps a hundred yards away. I am fed up with shells - they were all around me last night.

Things are going ahead all right. The 1/5th have done well. We got cut up - at least two companies did. Mason was the only officer out of them who was not hit. Old Fowler has been killed. I am cut up about this. I was with him up to the time he went to take up his position, as our two Companies were up while the two that got knocked about were resting.

I saw Leslie yesterday and Caley who is acting

adjutant saw him this morning. I am near where Tom has been situated but I've seen nothing of him though.

I understand the 8th have Cyril's pistol and case so possibly he's been buried. I hope to find more about this anon.

Wednesday 19th July 12 noon

I am in a wee place dug in to the side of one of the trenches. There are plenty of shells knocking around but one gets used to them as long as they are not too near. I had a near one last night. I took a bottle of rum to one of my platoons way down the trench. There was pretty heavy shelling. Stone, my servant, who acts as Orderly on these occasions was following near. A number of other troops were in the trench when we had shrapnel burst over us. A man between Stone and myself, and also one behind Stone, were killed and one or two others wounded, whilst we both got off scot-free. Stone did not know for a moment if he had been hit or not.

We got the rum through OK and we are back again here.

I shall have forty winks now - I seem to be able to sleep anywhere these days.

Thursday 20th July 10.15 am

I am all right but fagged out. It is good to be under canvas again. I shall sleep most of the day I bet.

Friday 21st July 3 pm

Well I am feeling quite well but I got gassed a little - a very little indeed thank you but I am quite fit. I had my jolly old helmet on in double quick time and so did Stone.

I am in a tent and the Divisional Band is playing just outside, so everything is quite merry and bright.

Saturday 22nd July 12.45 pm

I was very glad to get Peter's letter about Cyril - he was great. He could have come back twice but no, he kept on. I am wonderfully proud of him and knowing just what he must have gone through I can feel and know more than the folks at home.

The effects of the gas on me have dissipated - thanks to our helmets. None of my men have been lost.

I have been giving the Battalion some bayonet instruction. I wish I could give them more but we never stay long in one place.

Sunday 23rd July 12.30 pm

I am writing from down in a deep dugout. It is very much a better place than any I've been in in the old line. The enclosed printed letter will interest home and all the signatures are the officers present at the time we had the papers. Some are sadly now killed, some wounded but I must keep this letter.

The other is my report from the School. As one can see it is not all bad for me. It will be of interest to home.

The bally flies are beginning to get about again. They are a plague all over everything and everyone.

Monday 24th July 12.30 pm

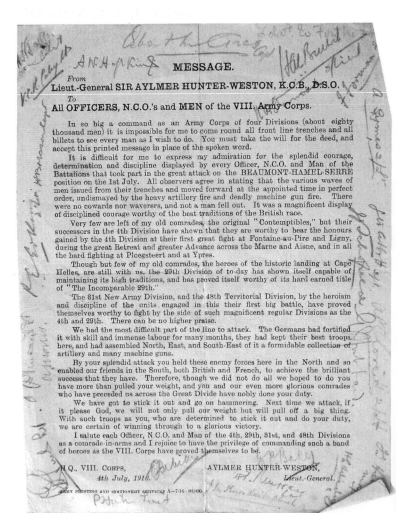

MESSAGE.

From
Lieut.-General SIR AYLMER HUNTER-WESTON, K.C.B., D.S.O.

To
All OFFICERS, N.C.O.'s and MEN of the VIII. Army Corps.

In so big a command as an Army Corps of four Divisions (about eighty thousand men) it is impossible for me to come round all front line trenches and all billets to see every man as I wish to do. You must take the will for the deed, and accept this printed message in place of the spoken word.

It is difficult for me to express my admiration for the splendid courage, determination and discipline displayed by every Officer, N.C.O. and Man of the Battalions that took part in the great attack on the BEAUMONT-HAMEL-SERRE position on the 1st July. All observers agree in stating that the various waves of men issued from their trenches and moved forward at the appointed time in perfect order, undismayed by the heavy artillery fire and deadly machine gun fire. There were no cowards nor waverers, and not a man fell out. It was a magnificent display of disciplined courage worthy of the best traditions of the British race.

Very few are left of my old comrades, the original "Contemptibles," but their successors in the 4th Division have shewn that they are worthy to bear the honours gained by the 4th Division at their first great fight at Fontaine-au-Pire and Ligny, during the great Retreat and greater Advance across the Marne and Aisne, and in all the hard fighting at Ploegsteert and at Ypres.

Though but few of my old comrades, the heroes of the historic landing at Cape Helles, are still with us, the 29th Division of to-day has shown itself capable of maintaining its high traditions, and has proved itself worthy of its hard earned title of "The Incomparable 29th."

The 31st New Army Division, and the 48th Territorial Division, by the heroism and discipline of the units engaged in this their first big battle, have proved themselves worthy to fight by the side of such magnificent regular Divisions as the 4th and 29th. There can be no higher praise.

We had the most difficult part of the line to attack. The Germans had fortified it with skill and immense labour for many months, they had kept their best troops here, and had assembled North, East, and South-East of it a formidable collection of artillery and many machine guns.

By your splendid attack you held these enemy forces here in the North and so enabled our friends in the South, both British and French, to achieve the brilliant success that they have. Therefore, though we did not do all we hoped to do you have more than pulled your weight, and you and our even more glorious comrades who have preceded us across the Great Divide have nobly done your duty.

We have got to stick it out and go on hammering. Next time we attack, if it please God, we will not only pull our weight but will pull off a big thing. With such troops as you, who are determined to stick it out and do your duty, we are certain of winning through to a glorious victory.

I salute each Officer, N.C.O. and Man of the 4th, 29th, 31st, and 48th Divisions as a comrade-in-arms and I rejoice to have the privilege of commanding such a band of heroes as the VIII. Corps have proved themselves to be.

H.Q., VIII. CORPS,
4th July, 1916.

AYLMER HUNTER-WESTON,
Lieut.-General.

ARMY PRINTING AND STATIONERY SERVICES A—746—81,000.

Letter from Lt. Gen. Sir Aylmer Hunter-Weston

170

Confidential Report - 4th Army Infantry School of Instruction

I am quite OK and kicking. At least I might be if this 'funk' hole - my present billet - was large enough.

I had a letter from Tom this morning - he seems well.

I am keeping merry all the time - of course no man alive can be told he's to take his company over the top in a hour or two and not feel twitchy. I haven't taken mine yet mind you, as it has fallen through each time for one reason or another, but we manage to get into some hot places now and again.

I will go and have a walk around now and see if the men are all right. They keep wonderfully cheerful and are always joking about something. The chief topic is about the possibility of a 'Blighty' one*. Abbot, one of my new subs, who is a fine fellow, has been hit by pieces of shell twice today and neither hurt him. He's quite fed up.

* FOOTNOTE: 'Blighty one' is a wound/injury serious enough to be sent home to England

Thursday 27th July 10.45 am

I have had a great time these last few days, right in the thick of things. I had a topping time bombing and I have revenged nearly all my pals. I will say more anon.

In 'The Story of the Royal Warwickshire Regiment (formerly the Sixth Foot)' by Charles Lethbridge Kingsford, published by Country Life Ltd, the following extract appears: *On 26th July, 1916 the 48th Division had helped in the important capture of Pozieres. The 143rd Brigade was in support; but Captain Hoskins and Lieut. Caley of the 7th Royal Warwickshire Regiment distinguished themselves by leading a brilliant little attack across the open.*

Captain Hoskins and Lieut. Caley were later awarded the Military Cross for this attack.

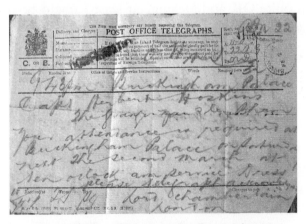

Post Office Telegraphs Investiture

Your attendance is required at Buckingham Palace on 2nd March at ten o'clock am. Service Dress. Please telegraph acknowledgement.

Lord Chamberlain, London

Saturday 29th July 2.15 pm

Poor old Edkins has been killed. He lay out wounded for two days. He was found on the second night but we did not expect he could live. He was a topping fellow and really loved his platoon.

I haven't yet been able to get further into the question of Cyril's body being found but I shall try and get over to see the 8th now and get some information.

Home will have seen by now where we've been as I noticed it in the paper. Those Anzacs are topping fellows. On one occasion they got so badly shelled in a line of the trench they had taken that they got fed up, so they walked over the top and took another where of course there was no shelling for a time.

I've got a few small things to give you. I have revenged my pals. It is a great feeling to have the running away in front of you. I can't tell you anything now but some day I will.

Pewter now displayed on Grandson's hearth -
'A few small things to give you'

Monday 31st July 3 pm

I went for a ride on Dick yesterday and saw Leslie, and I am going out again about 4.30 pm. This is a dead place - one must go somewhere in the evenings for a change.

We are working pretty hard. We've kicked against it but the Colonel is stubborn and can't see that after the last month or so we can all do with a slack time. It's jolly hot too - just the weather for the sea or the river at Stratford-upon-Avon.

Tuesday 1st August 1916 2 pm

It is very hot and at midday it is a job to find a cool spot anywhere.

Bayonets - I am jolly old Chief Instructor now. I had to take 'A' company today. The next thing will be to take the officers. Still it is useful to know that our of five or six officers who have been to the School, I am the first to get the CO keen about the bayonet. That course did wonders for me in the drill line.

There are some Battalion sports this afternoon from 3-7 pm and I may go for a spin on Dick afterwards.

Thursday 3rd August 1.45 pm

I hear today that Bushill may be back soon, which means that he will take 'D' again and I will go to 'A' I expect. I shall be sorry to move again now, having had these lads through the last show and training them now. Still, I will be glad to see Bushill back with us again.

Sunday 6th August 3.50 pm

A topping day and nothing to do except Church Parade this afternoon so I stayed in bed until ten, which made a nice change. I've been getting some straps with hooks made for use in connection with the Mills bomb. They seem to answer the purpose of pulling out the pins. Of course they will have to be proved in an actual stunt. Things so often turn out differently when used in practice at the back.

John (now Major Mellor) came in this morning, looking very pleased with life. He said he thought Tommy was somewhere not very far from here as some of the 14th were in a hospital close by. I will try and find out as I'd love to see him and I bet he'd be glad to see Your Humble.

Tuesday 8th August 6.30 pm

Charles Wade seems to have got a happy wound.

I see the 1st City Battalion have a number of names in the lists so perhaps they have had a rough time. Tom should be OK as long as he sticks to his cooker.

Friday 12th August 4.40 pm

We passed a gang of prisoners on the way here last night. They were working but not hard enough to please our men.

Thursday 17th August

I saw a plane toppled over by one of ours today! The old Bosh was swanking about nearly over our lines and it is not allowed. Our fellows are over their lines all day and night.

It's a very pretty place I'm in now - the trees are mostly splintered and the jolly old guns keep up a rain of shells - not on us, oh no - on the Bosh.

The flies!!! Never seen so many as in parts of the trench. Great big black and green fellows. I've got some gauze to cover my food and also a big piece for if I get a sleep by day to cover my face and hands.

Monday 21st August 8.10 pm

To tell the truth we've had rather a busy time the last few days. I am OK and my Company have done well. If there is anything in the papers I would like home to send me a copy. I should think there will be something.

Eric Murray was wounded on Saturday, so that is another of my pals gone away. Mason has been gassed just when he should have been taking his Company to support Payton, so I had to go up with my Company instead.

We have received one or two messages of praise recently saying that the way our Brigade went 'at 'em' was beyond all praise.

Following a night of rain (not cats and dogs but real live shells) - today is perfect.

Oh dear - a number of officers are being pulled up for sending news by letter - silly asses.

I am seated on my valise and I want home to keep an eye on the papers - Birmingham Post - for they will be reporting news of great interest.

Wednesday 23rd August 5 pm

News on leave. I am putting in a request for two weeks' extra leave and the Colonel has promised if we go back to forward it for me as 'strongly recommended'. I can't put in for leave while we are still here as I'd not like to be away when there are things to be done. There is a chance I may get back home soon in a week or so. Anyway the Colonel thinks I'll get away in a week.

Blast these flies - they are everywhere.

Sunday 27th August 6.30 am

I still hope for leave for next week. The Colonel seems to think I'll get away all right but the only thing is now that one of the men is wounded so I am the one and only Captain.

I saw John yesterday but only just had time to briefly tell him I have put in for special leave. His Colonel has water on the knee and I should think he's for Blighty, so John may have the Battalion for a while.

Tuesday 29th August 2.20 pm

My leave request went in yesterday and I know the Brigade has passed it on to the Divisional HQ so I stand a good chance of getting it and I may be home.

We've been in it again and I had the worst tour in I've experienced yet.

Caley, my sub, has just got the Military Cross. He's won it a dozen times over and I am just sorry it's not something more.

(Captain Hoskins was granted leave at the end of August 1916 and arrived home on August 31st. He was married to Caroline Marjorie Mellor in Birmingham on September 2nd. His best man was Henry Bushill. He returned to France from Charing Cross on September 8th.)

Wedding Day, 2nd September 1916
Groom: Herbert Hoskins, Bride: Caroline Mellor
Henry Bushell at back centre between
John Firth Mellor and Catherine Mellor.
Left of the groom is Laura Ellen Hoskins
Right of bride Dorothy Mellor (in VAD uniform)
Paige: John Jefferson - Bridesmaid Diana Davis.

Sunday 10th September 1 pm

I am back at the Battalion. I arrived here at 11 am. Everyone seems to have had the idea I was on three months leave! I am going over to see John after lunch. I have a message here to say he had put in for leave and wants to get any tips regarding the journey from me

Some Bosh propaganda has been dropped behind the French lines. Here is an example

German propaganda leaflet dropped over the French lines

Translation

French People!

Berlin, July 26 juillet 1916

Your aviators, dropping bombs, have killed men, women and children in great numbers over the last few weeks, far behind the front line, in the heart of Germany. In Karlsruhe alone on June 22nd 1916, there were 48 dead, among them 30 innocent children. Mullheim was bombed on June 22nd, Freiburg on July 16th, Kandern, Holzen and Mappach on July 17th, Heitersheimnear, Freiburg and Mullheim on July 22nd. All these raids resulted in many victims, dead or wounded. None of those places had any military importance, as anyone even without military competence can easily figure out just by glancing at a map.

German Command had first doubted that the French Government and its Generals would have been capable of such barbaric actions, which have nothing to do with conducting war. It believed that your pilots might have made a mistake in conducting their mission.

French People! *Your airmen were not mistaken! By pure chance we have uncovered the origin of these crimes!*

*We know today without the slightest doubt that they have been committed **under orders from your own government.***

Your President Poincaré himself has suggested this order, instigated by the

English with whom he shamelessly connived.

Just like you and us, the English know that the French People are tired of the many bloodbaths this war is costing. **Therefore something had to be done in order to reignite the anger and hatred against Germany.**

What better way to achieve that than to have your peaceful cities bombarded by German pilots? Well, in order to reach their goal, the English have designed this evil plan, to bomb Karlsruhe and other quiet neighbourhoods far from the front line. President Poincaré, **today England's puppet,** *to be deposed as soon as your flags will fold, was the immoral instrument of those actions.*

This is the plan as it was designed, and you are not to forget it was an English plan!

Germany fights the French Army, not the French civilian population, its women and children. Germany hopes that theses explanations will be sufficient to deter further similar barbaric attacks by the French aviation.

In case of further attacks, Germany would have no choice but to take similar actions to defend itself. Then you will know, French People, that **this serf to England Mister Poincaré,** *will be accountable for the bloodshed of innocent victims, and the English barbarians who will have forced us to wage destruction and death over your cities, far behind the front line.*

Wednesday 13th September 2.40 pm

It's a beast of a day so we have not been on parade yet. Still I can always find plenty to do as there is always some Company work that needs sorting. I went to see my old billet here yesterday and the folk were pleased to see me. This was Bushill's and Copper Murray's billet before.

There are several men getting Special Leave now and also a few of the men I am glad to say.

Monday 18th September 7.30 am

A perfectly wretched day. It rained all night and looks like doing so all day. We have a route march on.

Wednesday 20th September 6.25 pm

Rain all day on and off and everywhere is soaking and muddy. This war will go down in history. We managed to put in some drill this afternoon. I have no less than six officers now, including myself - one Scot (a very quaint little fellow) and three Welshmen. They all seem useful fellows.

There was some boxing after lunch before parade. We had it out in an orchard. The ground was soaking wet but it created some fun and there were one or two good rounds.

Two of the new officers had the gloves on. I concluded the show. At first no one seemed keen to take me on! I was very amused. Then they got a Lt. Cpl. to do so. He is a great big fellow about thirteen stone and we had a good spar I can tell you. Luckily for me he was not too good with the gloves so I was able to keep him in hand. Ha ha!

Monday 25th September

Have had a frightfully busy day and there is a big day on tomorrow and I shall be out all day from about 8 to 4.30 pm.

The CO has gone sick and so for the present I am second in command to Hanson. I guess Knox will most likely come out and take over soon.

Sunday 1st October, 1916 2.25 pm

We have returned to Old Time again and we all had an extra hour in bed and very nice it was too.

There is a battery of big guns some way from this billet and each time it fires it seems as though it is almost in the house. We are not right up yet so there is no need to worry ourselves too much.

We had a Communion Service this morning out in an orchard with the guns banging all around and the aircraft over us.

But it is a topping day and the sunshine has been really hot. It is a shame we have to be out here on such a job on these lovely autumn days.

Monday 2nd October. 3.50 am

The sun has gone in and it has turned out to be a wretched day. I've been soaked through. Holland and I rode over to Pas to get some money for the officers and also called and saw Marie. Holland - now acting adjutant - had not met Marie before. He's quite smitten.

Tuesday 3rd October 2.27 pm

The weather is a little better today but all the mud and slush with the rain on and off ensure the jolly old trenches will be in a state by now.

Thursday 5th October 10.20 am

As Second in Command one gets many small things to do and they crop up at all times. Still I am enjoying the job and it means I do not have the trouble of a Company to take care of.

I hear Field is out again so that is another old hand back and I am also informed that Bushill will be back soon, also Knox. But we do not expect them before the middle of this month.

John was in for tea today and his CO.

Saturday 7th October 9.30 am

I am sitting in Caley's dugout and using his pad while waiting for him to come in as I want to see him about a few jobs. It is nice to be back here and not a hundred yards away from our old winter quarters with everything much the same.

Our doctor has gone down sick - teeth trouble. It is the first time the poor doctor has gone sick since we came out.

Sunday 8th October 3.15 pm

We are all in huts which so far I am glad to say are watertight, although cold at night.

Wednesday 11th October 9.50 pm

I have been with Guest and Hicks to visit Marie this evening. She is only twenty next February. It was topping to be in the old room again, although I am about the only one left of the old original crowd who used to go.

Friday 13th October 9.45 pm

There has been an open air concert today combined with the 8th and it went off very well. Tomorrow we play the 5th at footer - weather permitting. I hope we whack them. We won against the 8th by three - nil.

The first of our wounded - Field - arrived back today . It is good to see him again. Just now in our mess I had all my old Company officers when I had 'A'. Gaussen, Hicks, Field and Caley. We are the only complete set left and we are all split up now.

Saturday 14th October 9.50 pm

We lost one-nil today against the 1/5th so we shall have to play them again and see if we can whack 'em then!

Monday 16th October 9.15 pm

We were only in the trenches the one night just around the corner from the spot we were in before.

Tuesday 17th October 10.15 pm

I have been in the 8th mess in the next hut since supper and am ready for my bed. It is raining again in fine style at present but most of this shanty keeps dry.

We have had a Battalion photo taken. I shall get prints at the end of the week.

Monday 23rd October 6.15 pm

I've got a swollen knee today. I was fooling about last night and strained it and now I am limping.

Two of my old 'D' Company men have been awarded medals. One a platoon sergeant and the other a stretcher bearer. There were four in our Battalion. I think D' is doing as well as any Company. That makes five and one officer (Caley)

I am now due at the 8th for dinner.

Thursday 25th October 12.5 am

The knee is improving but I still have a limp. I have only just got to bed and may be up early. I have had a rough day and am worn out. The Major has put his candle out so I must do likewise.

Friday 26th October 6.35 am

We have been on the move for two days. It rained during most of the march but my knee is better. We arrived at some huts quite empty and cold but have still managed to make ourselves more or less comfortable and I got to bed about 12. I have now developed neuralgia and had a poor night only to wake and find I have a cold also.

I have had to tell off three officers sharply since I have been on this job. After breakfast I was to ride and see a working party of ours but it was so bally cold it was hard work. I soon warmed up but it has not done my knee any favours. Now we have a stove going so things are improving.

Home would have loved to have seen what I have today - even to me it was wonderful. I mean our men are in tents where a few months ago No Man's Land was situated - and as far as one can see it is 'ours' and one can see a long way.

I have walked over a good piece of the ground. I can picture the fighting that took place and it was heavy fighting. Now it's all peaceful and hard to realise that only a month or two ago it was hell on earth.

Saturday 28th October 6.45 pm

Glad to say my head is quite well again and my cold better. I have obtained some liniment for my knee. A photo I sent may turn up in the Tatler - I am not sure - but if it does the folks are sure to see it.

Monday 30th October 6.30 pm

Mother has sent me an address of a man who says he's seen Cyril's grave, so I will get in touch with him at once. I hope its true.

The rain came down in torrents this afternoon - the front line will be in a pretty state again by now.

Damn this knee - I am afraid I overworked it yesterday.

Tuesday 31st October 5.45 am

A topping day with sunshine nearly all the while - such a happy change. I was out all morning seeing detached working parties.

There are heaps of prisoners working about the place. I feel like I'd like a good scrap with each. Some are fine big men so perhaps it's as well I can't!

Wednesday November 1st 9.50 pm

November! It has the sound of winter and at times feels like it as well. During supper last night a bomb fell near by and put our light out. The whole camp and all around was plunged into darkness. It fell though in an old trench and away from us all so no harm was done. It just caused amusement.

We soon settled down again but someone remembered the pudding and regretted it would be cold. Your Humble, though, had taken it to the kitchen to keep warm so we were soon able to continue as we left off.

Thursday 2nd November 7.40 am

I have been with John in his mess chatting for an hour so. It looks like we are for the mud again soon. There is plenty here but near the line it is 'some mud'. This war will be remembered for its mud.

Saturday 4th November 8.45 pm

We are in a little tin hut and sleep in a tent so we are quite all right. We have spent all day cleaning up the camp as the last folk left it very dirty.

I haven't any idea where Tom is - he writes that he is on HQ Company.

Two new officers have gone sick. The Major and I say we have been trying for twenty months to go sick and can't do it! I suppose a few of us here are now hardy enough to stand as much as anyone can. One does not notice it until these new fellows go crook.

The men generally are as hard as nails - I really do not know how they last. And somehow they always keep cheery. Our Brigade are jolly good fighters and excellent workers.

Monday 6th November 10pm

I have been jolly cold all evening but now with a good fire and a tot of rum I am just fine and feeling really warm all through and quite pleased with life - or perhaps I should say as pleased as one can be in this life.

The jolly old guns are bumping away merrily. We get a few back now and again but they are not too near. I wish we could have another slap at the Bosh as I am getting fed up being out. However I don't want trench life in these parts.

Yesterday we moved camp from a mud field to a green patch and a gale blew all the time so we had some fun putting up tents, bivvies etc. We all managed to get under cover before dark however.

I am sleepy now, caused by work (hmm!), the fire and the rum. I shall be gazetted as Temporary Major and draw pay for that time.

Knox should be here any time now. I could take off my crown but it is not worth it for so short a time.

Tuesday 7th November 9.30 am

This old shanty leaks quite well although we have a sheet spread all over the top. The tents are dry but there is no fire, so they are too cold to sit in.

We have had some rain the last few days - I guess we'll have to put up with plenty yet as well. I do not expect Knox to stand this weather for long. Last winter he was often ill and this winter looks like being a harder one.

Our old doctor left today and we have a new one.

Doc's gone to a field hospital. He's not ill but he has gone for a change. We shall miss him.

Wednesday 8th November 9.50 pm

It's raining again in fine style and the guns are popping off. Some game this! I think we are for the trenches in a few days.

Sunday 12th November 12.30 am

I am getting a bit fagged but I am still happy enough although dirty. I would just love a hot bath.

Bushill is out here now with a fellow called Iliff. The latter wrote to Hanson to say they would be here soon and wanted Hanson to apply for him to come to this Battalion, so in a few days I shall be Captain Hoskins again.

I have some big candles and one of them burned yesterday for 12½ hours and gave a really good light. They are really useful.

I fell into a shell hole last evening and at that time thought I'd a chance for Blighty but it really did me no harm - so no luck there.

Monday 13th November 3.15 pm

Bushill is at the Transport and - I cannot believe it - he's posted to the 1/8th. Of course he's furious but we shall get him back to us all right eventually.

Wednesday 15th November 12.15 pm

I am feeling very nice as I've had a wash this morning. I took my shirt and vest off for the first time in four days. It was very refreshing - one cannot imagine how much so until one has tried it.

Thursday 16th November 10 pm

Bushill will be here tomorrow. We've got him back all right. I do not know what the Colonel intends to do - I am trying to get him to put Bushill in for Major. Hanson will need to settle it tomorrow. He's out to dinner at the $1/8^{th}$ now.

Saturday 17th November 9.15 pm

The last two days have been very cold and frosty. I believe this time last year we had snow and I should not be surprised if we had some soon now.

Nothing has yet been settled about Bushill. He's sure to be our 2nd in a day or two. Hanson hoped to go on leave in a few days but he can't get away.

We had good luck this time in the trenches. No rain at all the whole time. We had quite expected to be living in mud.

There is a big gun handy here. Keeps going off and each time shakes the whole place. Keeps it up all the time - day and night.

Sunday 19th November 7.00 pm

I saw John this afternoon and we had a good chat. He walked part of the way back with me.

As predicted we had snow on the ground this morning, but all today has been wretched with rain and a cold wind. Our next tour in looks like being very sticky. What a war!

I go back to 'D' again tomorrow and shall put my three stars on again. Bushill can't put his crown up until it has gone through the usual course. At the same time I can't have crowns up with the 2nd in command as Captain. I do not mind giving way to Bushill but if it was anyone else I would be annoyed.

Some of us managed to get hot baths this afternoon. It was a pleasant change.

No news of Knox as yet except that the Division have applied for him.

The jolly old guns are all banging away in fine style just now. I hope they are having a happy time wherever they are falling. It's a rotten evening to get shelled.

Monday 20th November 11.50 am

I am back with 'D' Company. I spent all yesterday putting their mess in shape and organising a bed for myself. We are quite comfy. There is rather a large amount of fresh air - that one expects. At least I am writing at a table I made yesterday. There are also benches - the latter I have upholstered in sandbags.

I've got the shanty quite OK now with a wood fire on

the go. I hear there is an officer on the way up - that may be Knox.

The photo of the Battalion is in the Tatler I haven't seen it but they have at the Brigade.

At present we hope to be out and away by Christmas. It will be great if we are in billets away back. We shall have some time for Christmas but last year will take some beating.

Tuesday 21st November 5.35 am

I have now rigged up a fire with a pipe so that we can keep a good fire without being smoked out.

The guns are going strong just now. Someone is getting a thin time.

I hope to pop over and see John tomorrow if it is a decent day and there is not much going on.

Thursday 23rd November 5.30 am

I have some good news. I am going to our Divisional School for young officers as Instructor. With a bit of luck I will be there for some time. I was so surprised when I was told this afternoon. It will be a good change.

Bushill took over from me at once. He is well senior to me.

Sunday 26th November 2.50 pm

Colonel Harris, part of our Division has been in here to lunch and he says in the list of killed and wounded today that Bushill has been wounded. It must have been his first day in. They went in the night before I came here so perhaps I will have to return. I hope I may be able to remain here at least until they come out again.

Old Dr. Morris is here - a nice soft job for him and he tells me that Knox is still at Nuneaton and not likely to come out here yet!

I have a topping room here and a good bed, fire etc. It's such a happy change.

My job is to train and give lectures also. I am to smarten up the NCOs (all Corporals or Lt. Corporals). Another fellow has the offices, all junior. There are about thirty of each. I am glad I have the NCOs.

A typical day's work is as follows:

7 am - Physical training
9-12.45 pm - Field Engineering, Riveting and Trench digging.
2-2.45 pm- Lecture by Lt. Col. Marshall DSO, CRE
3-4 pm - Lewis gun instruction
6 pm - Lecture, DSC (Compass and Compass bearing)
(DSC - Discretion of Syndicate Commander

It is a full-time job. Also as in case of the 6 pm lecture I have to read it all up, so that means an extra hour or two. It means that one gets well polished up oneself of course. If I am not fetched back before the next School it will be easier for me.

It is rather strange to suddenly become an instructor. The Commandant here, a Colonel and a topping fellow, takes them all now and again to see how they are doing and I guess there would be some grouse if you hadn't improved them.

I am so fed up that Bushill has been wounded. Jolly bad luck. At present I do not know how badly wounded he is.

Monday 27th November 10.15 pm

I have not heard any more on my leaving here so perhaps I will be remaining. I am sailing along OK with my NCOs - there are some real good lads amongst them.

I do love my bed and to be able to sleep in peace and able to keep spick and span. What joy! A few weeks of this will do me a world of good.

Wednesday 29th November 10.30 pm

I learned yesterday that Knox has returned at last. Bushill was wounded in the leg by a piece of shell. Not very badly they think. Old Helsden was killed. He was a topping little fellow - I am very sorry indeed. Well now that Knox is back and Hanson only away on leave I do not expect to be recalled.

The Colonel here is very pleased with my men, so as long as Knox and Hanson keep fit and I satisfy the Colonel I may be here for some time - perhaps for Christmas.

Friday 1st December, 1916 9.50 am

The Commandant has passed all my NCOs for drill

except for four, but he said they were not too bad. Also he said he was delighted with the progress they had made. So that's good and it means I shall stay on as long as the Battalion do not send for me.

Next Course we hope to get things more shipshape. This being the first, things are not settled down. The next course will I believe start about the middle of next week.

Sunday 3rd December 3.15 pm

We have arranged for the next course today week, to have our own special subjects. There are two of us as Instructors. That will save a great deal of work. I have to read up a good deal as one has to be ready to answer any question.

We live in a château and I have a topping bedroom.

Monday 4th December 10.25 pm

School breaks up on Wednesday so I hope the next will be as good a set of men as these have been. It is very interesting to see them develop under one's tutorage. Some won't be recognisable when they get back to their Battalions.

Saturday 9th December 11.55 am

Bushill does not expect a trip back to Blighty. The doctor declares his wound will only take a few weeks.

Sunday 10th December 12.45 pm

My new students have turned up and look a useful enough set. The Commandant left yesterday to take Brigade for a while. I am sorry as I liked him. Still, the new one is a good chap so when we get used to him he'll be alright.

Thursday 14th December 12.40 pm

Spent the morning on a wiring demonstration. Oh but this class of officers - they are the limit! I'd like to have them for a month - one has not the time to tune them up in a fortnight. Really I didn't know we had such asses as some are.

This class is not such a game lot as the last - or so smart - but they are buckling down slowly.

Saturday 16th December 1.45 pm

Just heard the French have made a good push. It will make a good answer to old K. and his peace tricks.

I do not expect to get any leave yet - perhaps towards the end of January 1917.

FOOTNOTE: *The Imperial War Museum records show that Major Hoskins suffered three periods of illness. The first was in May 1915, when he suffered a dislocated cartilage in the kneecap at a sports day in Peronne. He suffered appendicitis in December 1917 and returned home on the Hospital Ship St. David in May 1917, by which time he was ranked Major. In July 1918 he suffered an unspecified illness (which may have been the effects of gas) which necessitated his return home. He was demobbed on 25th December 1918. Captain Hoskins was awarded the MC for conspicuous gallantry in connection with the important capture of Pozieres.*

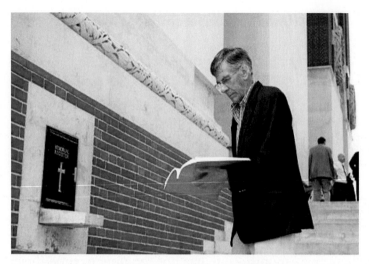

John Hoskins, Herbert's grandson, at Thiepval Memorial

Cyril's last letter home dated 24th June, 1916.

My dear Winn,

Many thanks for the topping parcel I received from London a few days ago. I am sorry that I have not written before but I am very busy indeed at the present time.

I hope that my little niece is progressing well, you did not say how she was in the note that was enclosed in the parcel.

You must be ready to receive any sort of news at any time and I hope you understand I cannot write any more on the subject.

'Old Brom' (Captain Hoskins) is still at school. He is due to return very soon now.

I don't know if you know that I am now O.C.B

Company and have been for the last month. I am getting one of the dogs now - ha, ha.

There really is nothing to write about - you know plenty on news but not for the people at home to know about - hard luck isn't it.

Cheer-O and much love
Cyril

'Goodbye old man'
Published by the Blue Cross Animal Hospital

HE whom this scroll commemorates
was numbered among those who,
at the call of King and Country, left all
that was dear to them, endured hardness,
faced danger, and finally passed out of
the sight of men by the path of duty
and self-sacrifice, giving up their own
lives that others might live in freedom.
Let those who come after see to it
that his name be not forgotten.

Lieut. Cyril Hoskins
Royal Warwickshire Regt.

Scroll in memory of Lieut. Cyril Hoskins,
killed in action 1st July, 1916

Lt. Cyril Hoskins

Son of John Ebenezer and Laura Ellen Hoskins. Born 26.9.1890.

Mobilised August 1914 1st/8th Battalion Royal Warwickshire Regiment

Killed in Somme battle 1.7.1916, aged 26. His body was not recovered.

Recorded by Imperial War Graves Commission 10.1.1929

Cyril's name is recorded on the Thiepval Memorial

THE WATCH DOGS XVIII
'Punch' 19th May, 1915

From Henry

My dear Charles,

It is now 2 am - an hour which I hope never to meet again when this business has ended; the rifles have quieted down, and both sides have abandoned, temporarily, the bellicose for the comatose attitude. I have just been leaning over the parapet contemplating in the moonlight that turnip field which separates us from our learned friends opposite, and is, in solid fact, an integral part of that thick black line of your newspaper maps, always so important-looking but so 'approximate only'. If turnip fields were capable of emotion this one would be filled with pride at the moment.

For generations it has been unnoticed and insignificant; its own tenant farmer may have been aware of its existence, but no one else probably knew or cared anything about it. And now there are some thousands of us whose whole attention, anxiety, enthusiasms, hopes and fears are concentrated on nothing else. It is sacred ground, on no account to be trodden on and hardly to be looked at by day and even in the dead of night only to be crept over with the utmost diffidence and respect.

We have sat on our respective edges of it for weeks, never taking our periscopes off it and reporting, as a matter of suspicion, the growth of every plant in it; and at the broken-down old cart which stands in the middle of it we have shot a hundred times (and so, no doubt, have they) as at a bold but crafty assailant.

Yesterday afternoon the field resumed, for a minute, some of its natural use. It was the after-lunch siesta; things were as peaceful as things can be in war; the sun shone and no sounds were heard except the casting of tinned-meat tins over the parapet - a form of untidiness, Charles, which Headquarters Staffs may rail against but are unable to check *personally*.

Suddenly the air was rent by the splutter of 'three rounds rapid' from the English trench on our left. From my dugout I heard, with grave anxiety, the firing being taken up by our own company; I was out and at the parapet just in time to see the solitary hare fall to the rifles of the company on our right... The man who had just slipped over into the forbidden area and recovered the corpse is, I take it, some *retriever*.

Our predominant feeling is one of intense curiosity as to what exactly is happening behind those black and white sandbags over the way. Are the Germans at this moment paraded there, being harangued by their officers before the attack, or are ninety per cent of them asleep and the other ten per cent, unmistakably yawning? Does the spiral of blue smoke ascending to heaven indicate a deadly gas manufacture or the warming up of a meat and vegetable ration? Are there ten thousand Germans there or ten? Are there, we ask ourselves testily after the long periods of inactivity which sometimes occur, are there any Germans there at all?

One of my men writes naively to his sweetheart:

'There's millions of Germans here but they's all behind bags'.

On the other hand, Lieut. Tolley, whose dashing spirits demand an attack, contends that the whole line opposing us has been deserted by the soldiery and is now held by a caretaker and his wife, the caretaker doing the occasional shooting, while his wife sends up the flare lights.

I write spasmodically between my rounds; I have just been questioning a sentry as to the formalities of his job. For instance, it is of the first importance that he should say, on the approach of the brigadier, 'No. 1 Post. All correct.' Even so he will no doubt get into trouble for something or other, but that remark, genially uttered, will help.

I ask my sentry what he has to do. 'Look out,' he answers. 'But suppose anybody comes?' I continue. 'Look out,' he says. 'But,' I press him 'if the Brigadier himself comes in to your bay and stands by you without saying anything, what will you do then'? 'Look out,' he repeated with feeling.

I take him next on the matter of less urgency. 'Suppose you see the enemy advancing from his trenches in great numbers, what will you do?' 'Shoot,' says he. I explain that two hundred rifles are perhaps more useful than one and ask him how he will give the alarm. The correct call is 'Stand to arms!' His, however, was nearly as good. 'I should shout, 'They'm coming!' said he.

They are now starting this artillery business at night, which is really rather tiresome of them. You may imagine correct." Even so, he will no doubt get into trouble for something or other, but that remark, genially uttered, will help. I ask my sentry what he has to do. "Look out," he answers. "But suppose anybody comes?" I continue. "Look out," he says. "But," I press him, "if the Brigadier himself comes in to your bay and stands by you without saying anything, what will you do then?" "Look out," he repeated with feeling.

I take him next on a matter of less urgency. "Suppose you see the enemy advancing from his trenches in great numbers, what will you do?" "Shoot," says he. I explain that two hundred rifles are perhaps more useful than one and ask him how he will give the alarm. The correct call is "Stand to arms!" His, however, was nearly as good. "I should shout, 'They'm coomin'!'" said he.

They are now starting this artillery business at night, which is really rather tiresome of them. You may imagine how, in an artillery duel, one lot of guns, not knowing where the other lot is, gets tired of looking. But there is always the day's ration of shells to be got through. I have no doubt it is the same with the Germans as with ourselves; what with certificates, reports and returns, it is much less tiring to shoot away all the darned stuff than to keep any by you unexpended. And so the gunners look, after a while, for their customary target, its whereabouts fixed and known. Churches, houses, windmills and the like are everywhere limited, and here they have all been used up long ago; but there is one target always there, always vulnerable and always ready to rebuild itself when hit. Yes, Charles, from the German gunners' point of view that target is Us, and so over come the shells with a slithering, genial whistle, as if to say, "Do just come out of your hole and watch the burst." We have lost fifteen new-laid eggs, a dozen mineral water and a farmhouse clock in yesterday's encounter; and, after it was all over, no doubt those infernal gunners of ours, who had started the row, retired to their dug-outs away back behind the line, and had an omelette lunch.

The topic reminds me of our industrious but incompetent mess waiter, Private Blackwell. If ever a man in this world meant well but missed it he does. You have only to whisper his

name and he bursts into the mess hut like a whirlwind, dropping knives and forks, tripping over chairs, sweeping crockery off the table, in his uncontrolled enthusiasm. To enable himself to get through more work he leaves the table with just twice what any man could carry, and drops it all before he gets to the door. This dropping has become a fixed habit with him; he drops everything, however heavy or light, fragile or valuable, but through accidents and abuse he maintains his cheery department of impulse and impetus.

A week ago we were all of us sitting

SUGGESTIVE BACK VIEW GIVEN SHORT-SIGHTED SPECIAL
THE THRILL OF HIS LIFE (BUT IT WAS MERELY A CHAUFFEUR
PREPARING TO ENJOY AN EXTRA FINE BANANA).

round the mess table at midnight, having just returned from a period in the trenches—a moment when we suffer a little from the want of sleep and the reaction after the nervous tension. Suddenly the door flung wildly open, and in burst the ecstatic Blackwell, carrying ("Heaven defend us!" shouted the Adjutant) an enormous shell. "But, of course," we reassured each other, "it is only the empty case." "No, Sir," declared the bearer, hustling over all obstacles to the C.O. at the far end of the room, "it fell by Trench Headquarters just before we left, and hasn't burst yet." Never in my life shall I forget the sensation caused by that "yet"!

For the rest, "Cheer-oh!" (as one of my platoon writes), "we 'll learn them German chaps to keep on their own doorstep."   Yours,   HENRY.

UNDESIRABLE POSES.

[Several of our photographic newspapers recently had a picture of the CHANCELLOR OF THE EXCHEQUER resting on the heather at Walton Heath after a round of golf. A medical correspondent wrote to The Daily Mail criticising the CHANCELLOR'S rashness. "He was risking an attack of lumbago, rheumatism, loss of voice, or even some much more serious consequence of sudden chilling of the heated body. To lie on the grass at this time of year in the case of a man over forty is a very risky proceeding."]

WE feel that it is time that expert criticism was directed towards other pictures in our illustrated newspapers, and we print one or two comments we have received in reply to instructions issued to our own corps of specialists.

"The photograph of that charming actress, Miss Cissie Cinnamon, in The Daily Sketch, exhibits a recklessness which in after years this lady is likely to deplore. The highest dental authorities agree that, while it is necessary that the teeth should be exposed occasionally to prevent them from turning yellow, the chemically tainted atmosphere of a photographer's studio is most harmful to both ivory and porcelain."

"No wonder the recent poems of Mr. Alvescar Annalane have shown a falling off. The reason is to be seen in a portrait of this gentleman which is printed in The Daily Sketch. He is posed with his hand against his face, his forefinger pressing against his temple. Pressure in this place cannot fail to interfere with the proper operation of an important artery whose duty it is to feed the brain, and its obstruction must result in an impoverishment of thought."

"The full-length portrait of the popular young composer of 'We'll make the KAISER sit up in the morning!' which appears in The Morning View, reveals that this young man is not aware of the rudiments of a correct military posture (for we assume from his work that he has the military instinct). The heels should be together and in line, the feet turned out at an angle of about forty-five degrees; the knees should be straight; the body should be erect, the arms hanging easily from the shoulders with the thumbs immediately behind the seams of the trousers, the hands being partially closed. The head should be steady, the eyes looking their own height and straight to the front."

how, in an artillery duel, one lot of guns, not knowing where the other lot is, gets tired of looking. But there is always the day's ration of shells to be got through. I have no doubt it is the same with the Germans as with ourselves; what with certificates, reports and returns, it is much less tiring to shoot away all the darned stuff than to keep any by you unexpended.

And, so the gunners look, after a while, for their customary target, its whereabouts fixed and known. Churches, houses, windmills and the like are everywhere limited, and here they have all been used up long ago; but there is one target always there, always vulnerable and always ready to rebuild itself when hit. Yes, Charles, from the German gunners' point of view that target is US and so over come the shells with a skittering, genial whistle as if to say 'Do just come out of your hole and watch the burst.'

We have lost fifteen new-laid eggs, a dozen mineral waters and a farmhouse clock in yesterday's encounter; and, after it was all over, no doubt those infernal gunners of ours who had started the row, retired to their dugouts away back behind the line and had an omelette lunch.

The topic reminds me of our industrious and incompetent mess waiter, Private Blackwell. If ever a man in this world meant well but missed it he does. You have only to whisper his name and he bursts into the mess hut like a whirlwind, dropping knives and forks, tripping over chairs, sweeping crockery off the table, in his uncontrolled enthusiasm. To enable himself to get through more work he leaves the table with just twice what any man could carry and drops it all before he gets to the door. This dropping has become a fixed habit with him; he drops everything, however heavy or light, fragile or valuable, but through accidents and abuse he maintains his cheery deportment of impulse and impetus.

A week ago we were all of us sitting round the mess table at midnight, having just returned from a period in the trenches - a moment when we suffer a little from the want of sleep and the reaction after the nervous tension. Suddenly the door is flung wildly open and in bursts ecstatic Blackwell carrying ('Heaven defend us!' shouted the Adjutant) an enormous shell. 'But of course,' we reassured one another, 'it is only the empty case.' 'No, Sir,' declared the bearer, hustling over all obstacles to the CO at the far end of the room, 'it fell by Trench Headquarters just before we left and hasn't burst yet.'. Never in my life shall I forget the sensation caused by 'yet'.

For the rest, 'Cheer-o' (as one of my platoon writes) 'we'll learn them German chaps to keep on their own doorstep.'

Acknowledgements

'The Watch Dogs' PUNCH May 19th 1915
Reproduced by kind permission of
Punch Ltd. London W1K 1NA

Old photographs of the Great War: www.gwpda.org.

The Imperial War Museum, London.

'Gloves on'
'Bayonet Practice'
'Roll Call in the Trenches 1st July, 1916'
'British Officer making nights rounds in the Trenches'

Nick Fear, History Research Service, www.nickintime.co.uk

Painting 'Goodbye old man' by J. Matania,
reproduced from the Blue Cross War Horse Collection,
courtesy of The Blue Cross, Animals Hospital, London
Reg. Charity no. 224392

Thanks to Didier and Veronique Requena for interpreting the
propaganda leaflet dropped over the French lines.

Chris Newton of Memoirs Books thanking him
for his patience.

Photographs

Jam pot bomb and Lemon bomb (mock-ups)
can be found at the Royal Regiment of Fusiliers Museum
(Warwick), St John's House, Warwick CV34 4NF,
charity no. 272357

Special thanks to artist Jan Harvey for her clever sketches.
I am certain my grandfather would have appreciated
her interpretation.